On the Road Again

Jeff,
The experience of being in Telling: Gainesville & working with you was a gift to me.
Thank you,
Sue Dudley

ON THE ROAD AGAIN

*Stories from an Air Force Pilot's Wife
(1953-1974)*

(Epilogue to 2003)

Sue Coffman Dudley

Copyright © 2017 Sue Coffman Dudley
All rights reserved.

ISBN: 1539315045
ISBN 13: 9781539315049

The Beginning

Tucson, Arizona, 1954
Selma, Alabama, 1955

This was the worst date of my life, I thought, almost in despair. *Now, I know why my sorority at Mizzou (University of Missouri) refused to let its pledges date anyone from our local military base--you could end up hiding out in a bathroom. What a mess!*

"Don't make excuses, Sue," I said, giving the gleaming white wall a kick for emphasis. "You need to remember that a summer session at UA (University of Arizona) was your idea of an adventure." Leaning back against the cool white tiles, I quietly chanted: "It's okay. You're okay."

This was my first week at UA, and I had been piling up all sorts of new experiences. To calm myself I began to list them: seeing my first orange on a tree, my first sight of a white person and black person together as friends, sleeping outdoors in the screened-in-porch on the front of my dorm, and--something that was forbidden at Mizzou--girls wearing shorts on campus.

The smell of some sort of cleanser made me move away from the bathroom wall. "Make sure you add tonight's date to your list," I muttered, as I kicked the wall again in disgust.

The girls in the dorm had been treating me like a pet monkey as they enthusiastically worked to reprogram a curious, shy, unsophisticated eighteen-year-old from a small lead-mining town in the foothills of the Ozark Mountains. They insisted that I go on this blind date with a cadet from nearby Marana, Air Force Base. They pushed me out the door. And when I fussed, they repeatedly told me: "You just don't understand it here. These guys are going to be officers and pilots. And, they are soooo cute!"

This was why I found myself, just outside of Tucson, in the public bathroom of a resort on top of Mt. Lemmon trying to stay away from an obnoxious date. Now would be a good time, I decided--as I looked in the little bathroom stalls to see if I could find some way to be comfortable and private--to seriously think about the unusual actions of my family that got me here.

My summer's adventure had been born in the pledge Liz and I made to be friends forever. After her father's death, Liz had lived for several years in my hometown of Flat River, Missouri, pop. 5,400. Then, when we entered our junior year of high school her stepfather's health required her family to move to Prescott, Arizona. The fall we both entered college, I picked MU's new five year program that would have me graduating as a registered Nurse with a Bachelor of Science. Liz picked a girl's school near Mizzou; she said to be close to me.

The new experiences that would end up rerouting my life were started by Liz insisting that I should to go to Arizona that year for my summer classes--to visit her. That being only fair, I simply asked Mom and Dad. With no conversation and no discussion, they gave a very, very unexpected "Yes."

This was only a month before UA started their summer session. Since Mizzou would be in finals at the same time UA's summer sessions began, I'm rearranging what finals I can, and bailing out of Chemistry because that professor would not give his test early. Then, bang, I'm on my very first air plane and going to Tucson.

Honestly, it had never occurred to me that my parents would grab that moment and send me off to Arizona. And, their decision was more than a surprise coming from what I *thought* was my family background.

Life in our house was very quiet, and revolved around my father. In the summer, after work, he would garden and go to bed early. Winter evenings, every year, were spent with my mother quietly doing some sort of embroidery while Daddy read his books out loud to me.

The year my father was reading *Northwest Passage* by Kenneth Roberts, I taught myself to read by deciphering the next page. This was in 1940, and that was all I had to do as I spent most of the winters of my fifth, sixth and seventh years in bed. For months, I had to use a bedpan; I wasn't even allowed up to go to the bathroom.

The doctors said I had rheumatic fever because I had a low grade fever, heart murmur and joint pain. All my symptoms seemed to disappear every summer. After three winters of bed, revolving doctors and medications, I think my frustrated mother decided to give up. She started ignoring me; and, I got better.

The gift that I got from all this crazy business was an early passion for stories and information. For the rest of my childhood, anything I knew about adventures, excitement, or the world would come from books. I obsessively read out the libraries in Flat River and all the towns around us.

Our family could have been described as poor except everyone was poor in Flat River. Before I was born in 1935, Daddy had been appointed postmaster by Franklin Delano Roosevelt. This meant he didn't work in the lead mines, and I thought that was what seemed to set us apart.

My father kept a perfect, pleasant family. There were absolutely no arguments, and very little laughter. We had only small upsets. One time, my mother said "Damn!" when she poured hot grease on her hand while cooking. For privacy, Daddy took her into the bathroom for a lecture. I never heard another bad word in my family. Once, I used the word "sex" in our house, just in a sentence, and got taken into the bathroom for my lecture.

Daddy, a happy, charming fellow, was completely unable to hear, or to understand, that a child of his might not want what he did. Another small example of my childhood frustration was that I never had slaw that he didn't put gravy on it. I sputtered that I didn't want gravy. I tried everything I could think of within the bounds of my small world to stop him. But, at our required family supper table this scene played again and again: smiling as he served my plate he would cover my slaw with gravy, saying, "Few white men and no niggers ever have anything as fine as this."

As I grew up, I simply quit talking at home about most things--and read more books.

It was in the 9th grade that I began to rebel. We all did, the group of five girls that I grew up with. Schneider and Anne were older; Sarah, Janet and I were a year behind them. (I was the last in the group to mature physically, and the quietest.)

What we did was start smoking. As my mother never came into my bedroom, it didn't occur to me to hide the cigarettes. One day, Mother found them. Not saying a word, she waited for my father to get home from work. Then they went into the bathroom and shut the door. I could hear my mother's frustrated voice: "Roy, what do you think she's doing?" All my father said, over and over again, was "My daughter does not smoke." That was it. The five of us continued smoking, stupidly thinking we hid our behavior. But, in my family not one thing about it was ever again said to me.

I began to think that in our house my father created his world the way he wanted it. It would be a very long time before I began to understand that he created his world the way he *needed* it to be.

Secrets supported the simplicity of my father's world--secrets that the whole town kept.

Somewhere in my late 30s, I began to look at my 'growing-up' differently. It was in Flat River one Christmas. I was telling my brother, Charles, about an older boy in our town: the Sheldon boy. "He was always there. When I walked home late at night, he was a block behind. If a group that I was in started to get rough at a basket-ball game, or anywhere, he walked in, and it dispersed. He just--was. I don't think I ever spoke to him. He was considered tough, and ended up in the penitentiary."

"That's odd," said Charles. "That was a big family, and one of the older kids did the same thing for me."

Daddy had been listening, intensely. "I may know why," he said. "After Roosevelt was elected, I got a phone call. They wanted to know if I would hire the people for the CCC (Civilian Conservation Corps) to build the roads and sidewalks in Flat River. I walked our town and asked the men that I knew who needed work if they wanted a job. Mr. Sheldon told me later that his family had not eaten in three days. They were on their knees praying to God to help them when I knocked on his door."

Most of the people in Flat River were tough, stoic, Ozark hill people. They thought in terms of family. And, if they owed you, it really meant something. This was a gift silently given to me. Sometimes it was fun. Often on hot summer nights, when we were supposed to be sleeping on one of our family porches, my friends and I would walk the town around 3 or 4 a.m. Pounding on bakery or ice cream factory doors (I was never the one pounding) would bring a very mad someone to stop us. All the angry words would cease as they noticed me--my red hair was distinctive. "You're the little Coffman girl, ain't ya?" Then we would be given big smiles along with donuts, or cookies, or pints of ice cream.

One afternoon in the country, we found a train slowly chugging up the hill. Schneider whooped and grabbed for the ladder on the side of a moving car, then we all jumped the train. The engineer saw us. Bringing the train to a grinding stop, he came back in a fury to break some heads. Noticing me, my hair again, he said: "You're the little Coffman girl, ain't ya?" Then he let us run the train forward and back while we took turns blowing that mournful horn.

It wasn't until I was in my 50s that I began to emotionally understand my father's total focus on everyone else's opinion.

That was when I finally found out that the family story Daddy had told his children about his father was not true. We were told that our grandfather sold the family farm to St. Joseph Lead Company for $7,500--that it was so much money he told St. Joe to keep the $500--then Grandpa drank himself to death. In reality, after the farm was sold, Dad's mother and father were divorced. This was in 1897.

That was the year Daddy, the last child of this family, was born. (There were nine children, and the closest child was Leeman, seven years older than my father. I never knew any of the others.) What was more than astonishing about this story was the whole town kept my father's secret. My grandfather, his new wife and new children, lived within fifty miles of Flat River. I may have passed cousins on the street. Not one word ever, ever got out to my two older brothers or to me about this.

My mother knew everything, but she was a stoic, and silent. Mom believed that you did what you were supposed to do. Her father was a Presbyterian minister, YMCA director, and fly fisherman. Her mother was a very fine amateur artist. All Mom's family were intelligent, but some had an odd, adventurous quirk.

For my mother, I think her third pregnancy, with me, was a terrible blow. She was thirty-five years old, my brothers ten and seven. My father got a redheaded, brown-eyed little girl that the people in town could pet. Then, he expected my mother, who was unimpressed as her whole family had the same coloring, to change her life to take care of me. I can't imagine how dull her world must have become.

I don't think she knew how to play. A nurse of the old school, she did not believe in holding children as that would spoil them. She did not hug me, or touch me, or sympathize over cuts, or sunburn, or spend any time talking to me. I was shocked as an adult to find out that before I was born she used to play bridge, that she had gone to Garden Club meetings, and she had friends over for dinner. In my growing up years in Flat River, I can count on one hand the times someone came into our house for a cup of coffee or to socialize in any way.

It must have been more difficult than I can begin to understand. I was in Oklahoma when Mom and Dad sold the house. Mom phoned, and said, "I'm going to dump everything on the sidewalk. You better come." When I got home, she was on the back lot standing by a fire--silent and unapproachable. My mother was burning everything she could: papers, letters, her wedding certificate, family pictures. "I have been tied down to things all my life," she said. "Not anymore." She left the house I was born in with a small cranberry bowl that had belonged to her mother.

My mother didn't enter my world that I knew of, until I graduated from high school. Then, as I found out much later, she silently stepped in with surprising strength.

The changes coming into my life were triggered by as simple a matter as getting my father to let me go on a high school band trip. It was like talking to a pleasant, empty robot. I couldn't stop trying, insisting the impossible: that he hear me. It was, to me, so emotionally difficult that I stood before him in the dining room and vomited in my hands. My mother, a statue framed in the kitchen doorway, watched this scene without any expression. Then she said, "I think it's time you left home." Right there a new door to my future opened. That summer as I left for St. Louis to work at a bank and share an apartment with friends, my father cried. In the fall I entered Mizzou; late the next spring, in Tucson, I started summer school at UA.

"Sue, are you alright? Your date sent me in here to check on you. I think he's feeling lonely. Are you sick?"

"Donna, just a little nauseous," I said, quickly putting my feet on the floor of the bathroom stall where I had managed to find a way to make myself comfortable while I thought about my life. "I'll be out in a minute." As I heard the door close, I came out of the little potty room. "Well, I guess I'm through hiding," I said to the tall red head reflected in the mirror. Feeling better, I tugged the bathroom door open and went out into the hall.

"Hey, Donna, you didn't have to wait for me."

"I got you to come on this blind date; and, he does seem a little pushy. Sure you're all right?"

"This guy does not want to hear no. Maybe it will help if I give him some more time off while I make certain my stomach's settled. I'll be back in a while," I said, and moved off into a darkened ballroom.

I walked over to the large window that framed an amazing picture, at that moment all in black and grays, of the mountains and their forest of pine and fir. Just then a huge moon came out from behind the clouds and golden light poured over the trees. It was magic. "Oh! Look! This is just wonderful!" I said, of the view, and to the tall, young man standing there.

"Yes, it is," he said, as he turned to me with a smile in his beautiful eyes.

And, I was in love.

Dudley, who was also a "pilot in training" at Marana, knew all the guys. He attached himself to our group, and to me in particular, with such enthusiasm that I moved back and forth from embarrassment to delight.

After that evening, I waited two long miserable weeks for a phone call. Finally, Dudley called. He talked for one hour and hung up. It was another week before we had a date--and that was the last time I ever went out with anyone else.

Dizzy with exposure to all the healthy hormones and testosterone suddenly available, I would wait uncomplaining for hours on a weekend to see if Dudley could get in from Marana. This wasn't often as he was usually in trouble and spent great blocks of time walking off demerits. These guys all thought they were born to be fighter pilots. They thought it was fun to buzz the Grand Canyon. They loved to scare the bejesus out of train engineers by flying straight at an on-coming train, "on the deck" as they would say--pulling up at the very last minute.

On the weekends, these beginning pilots would just show up in our dorm Commons Room. One afternoon, hoping Dudley could visit, I spent my time watching a tall, very good looking, senior girl interact with them. It turned out to be a lifetime gift for me. Her name was Josh; and, she had more "presence" than anyone I had ever met. As young men, most of them looking lost, walked into the room, she would move toward them, comforting and awesome in her confidence, stick out her hand, and say, "Hi! I'm Josh."

Amazing, I thought, as I watched, over and over again, those faces light up in relief--reflecting the glow of that personality and greeting. Looking back on my life, I don't know how many rooms I've entered, or new people I've met, where, from my memory I have copied her walk and confidence.

My summer sessions were over, and this was to be a special motel weekend. Liz was here to pick me up so I could spend five days with her in Prescott. With my encouragement, she had found a room of her own. It was my last night in Tucson and Dudley and I had planned to spend it together. With all the romance in my eighteen-year-old soul, I had decided to give my virginity to him as a gift. As it turned out, we were both virgins. The experience was naive, charming--and wonderful!

Liz charged into our room the next morning demanding to know Dudley's intentions. And, he laughed.

On my bus ride home to Flat River from Liz's home in Prescott, I cried and cried knowing that I had had a summer romance; it was over. When I got home, there were five letters waiting for me, and hope bloomed.

Now, it was Thanksgiving; and Dudley was coming. I was a mess, thinking: What will happen when he sees me again? Will it be all right? What will we talk about? How can I get rid of my parents? I was so excited and scared that I was nearly sick, desperately wanting to be alone when I met him for the first time since Tucson.

Mom and Dad had been in Kansas City with my brother Charles, as his wife was having their first child. They picked me up at Mizzou, and we drove to St. Louis to get Dudley. Somehow, I talked my father and my silent disapproving mother into taking the three-hour bus ride home from St. Louis while I took

11

the car to the train station to get Dudley. The minute I saw him, walking toward me in his too small high school athletic sweater and big smile, I knew everything was all right. After kisses, very tight hugs, and some tears from me, Dudley said, "Where's your Mom and Dad?"

"Oh! What have I done?" I said, with a sinking heart and guilt overwhelming me. "I left them at the Greyhound station to get a bus home."

"You didn't!" Dudley looked at me in horror. "Oh! God! I haven't even met them yet!" He grabbed my hand and started to run. "Where is it? Maybe we can get there before the bus leaves." We raced for the station. And there they were, sitting glumly side by side on a bench with another hour to wait before they could even get a bus home. I watched, amazed, as this young man I adored managed, with his easy southern charm, to make everything all right.

A month later, when Dudley arrived for Christmas, I saw the besotted faces on my mother and father when we walked into the house from the bus station and he said, "Hi ya, Sport," and "Hi Honey!" I had never heard anything like this in my life, and neither had they; the effect was stunning. The combination of brashness and southern warmth melted, for him, the stiffness, properness, and reserve that structured the family shell I grew up in.

All my dreams of a college education happily flew away with my Christmas gift: a little ring with diamonds in it. I left Mizzou at the end of that fall semester as my mother said I had to learn how to cook.

In April, Dudley, now in Phoenix, got his wings; and I flew out to pin them on. Mother had given orders that we were not to drive back together if we weren't married. "If my assignment is fighters," Dudley said, "it's too dangerous, and we won't get married. If I get something else, we will." Orders came for school in Selma, Alabama– then on to Webb, AFB, Big Spring, Texas as an instructor in T-33s.

We were married in the judge's chambers of the courthouse in Phoenix, Arizona. As court was in session, we walked by a gauntlet of strange, scruffy-looking people sitting on the floor along both drab gray walls of the hall waiting for their turn before the judge. All seemed to want to attend our wedding, and they all made comments: "Honey, are you getting married?" "Oh! Can I come?" "Ain't she sweet!" "Go for it Guy! Do your duty!"

The day after Dudley's graduation, we started our drive to Selma. The wife of his flight instructor had invited us for a wedding breakfast before we left. I was shy and didn't quite know what to do when I found a young man sleeping in her bathtub. "Oh, ignore him. I often have someone in the bathtub," she said, beginning the lessons from a sisterhood that I would not understand for some time but was now a part of. "I was afraid for him to drive home last night," she added, as she handed me a wedding gift: an address book. "Promise me that you will never write in it in pen. Your friends will move around a lot--always write in pencil so it is easy to erase." I promised, and kept both the vow and the book for the next twenty years.

There were lots of changes. A silly one was surprisingly difficult. I obviously couldn't call Dudley Dudley any more even if it felt right. Everyone called him Dudley; and we had been dating for several weeks before I found out it wasn't his first name. Ronald just didn't work, so I began to use R.D.

One of those changes was important. I hadn't noticed that I had quit drinking coffee, but R.D., a non-smoker, noticed that I had stopped smoking. When my stomach started acting up, R.D., concerned, sent me out to the base medical center for a check-up. There, a bored nurse gave me a B vitamin shot, patted me on the head, and muttered, "Congratulations you're pregnant."

All the young wives of these new pilots were pregnant. Because a bunch of our husbands were assigned to Webb, we were delighted to find out one of the older wives was from Big Spring. I gave a coffee. "Tell us," we said, sitting on the floor around her chair like an arraignment of brightly colored balloons, "about our new home."

"Well," she said, "this is west Texas; you're pretty isolated. Midland is the nearest town; and it's forty miles away. At this time, there isn't any base housing, and they are just building an Officer's Club." Young, naive, excited, we sat there mesmerized as she continued. "Sand storms have become a problem as a drought has been in effect for eight years. A light plane crashed between the runways during a storm some months ago, and no one even knew about it for twenty-four hours."

This news about our next base didn't dampen my spirits. I think it was beginning to dawn on me that instead of reading about an exciting life, I might have a chance to live one. Besides, at that time, I was more focused on my sick stomach. R.D. had been shaving each morning bravely trying to ignore me vomiting whatever I could into the potty. As I look back, I think with a smile that the trip from Selma to Big Spring was a perfect beginning to the rest of my military adventures as a pilot's wife. On our drive across the country, R.D. didn't even stop the car, he just slowed down, and I hung out the open door and threw up--the entire trip to Texas. Life was great! Nothing was going to interfere with our excitement. We were on our way!

Baby Becky

Big Spring, Texas, 1956

I was twenty years old; I was going to have a baby in six weeks; and, I had come to the conclusion that I might die. This was ridiculous, the conclusion I mean, for I had planned on being a nurse. Typical of me, I could name the hormones and stages of a baby's prenatal development; I knew where babies came from; but I knew nothing about having one. I had never even held a baby.

We were living in Big Spring, Texas, where R. D. taught flying at Webb AFB. My mother and father had come to see us for the three-day visit that was all my mother ever allowed them to stay. I needed to tell someone about my fear. I wanted someone to hold me, someone to say everything would be all right. Against my better judgment, I picked my mother. Scared, sick to my stomach, ashamed and in tears, I told my mother that I was afraid. She let me get it all out as she stood framed in a doorway of our small apartment, her brown eyes flat with displeasure. "You don't think," she said, "you are the first woman who has had a baby, do you?"

Well, that's that, I thought. *If I die, I die.* So, I shut up.

It was very exciting when I started contractions. R. D. took me out to the base clinic where the doctor said, "You've dilated. Go to the hospital." R.D. took me home to pack a bag, and to the library to get some books. Then we went to a friend's house where we borrowed two dollars to go get root beer ice cream floats to celebrate.

Ronald dropped me off at the hospital and said he would be back that evening. The contractions got stronger but I felt fine. I ate my dinner and the dinner of another mother-to-be, who was my roommate. By the time R. D. left that evening, I was getting depressed. I walked the halls and tried jumping a little for I was sure it was false labor, and they would send me home the next day.

My roommate was a mess, hollering and carrying on, so they took her away fairly early. Later, as my contractions got harder, a nurse running through asked me if I wanted anything. "No," I said, trying to get my breath as I grunted.

This must have been a pretty busy night because a doctor ran in the room, gave me a shot of something, jerked up the bars around my bed, and ran out. The two dinners made me sick. I kept banging my head into those bars trying to get over to the side of the bed as I threw up. At some time that night, the doctor and nurse showed up to take me into the delivery room. "Just give me a minute," I said, "while I get through this push."

"Like Hell!" the doctor said, as he grabbed me and threw me on the gurney. "You're having a baby!"

So, I did...

I was sobbing my heart out the next morning when a nurse came in with Becky. "What's the matter, dear?" she said.

"My husband hasn't come to see me."

"What!" she said, as she stomped out to rectify this little problem. R.D. showed up fairly soon after that. No one had called him to tell him he had a little girl.

That night when the nurse came in she told me the doctor said I was wonderful; I didn't make a sound. He told her that if all women were like this one, being an OB doctor wouldn't be so bad. I snorted, and thought, *They all should have my mother.*

I woke and went to sleep hearing my daughter cry. The nurses kept her out of my room as much as possible. They would quietly mention to me that she cried a lot. Being a baby seems to be tough, I decided.

My mother, who had been a nurse, came to help because I had a blood clot in one leg from the birth. The next morning when Becky started screaming, I got out of bed, and charged to the rescue--only to find my mother bathing her. She was holding my baby like a sling, Becky's two baby hands in one large hand, and her two baby feet in the other large hand. Mother was rinsing my baby by swinging her back and forth under the running water of the kitchen faucet. Then she laid Becky down on the drain board. Horrified, I gathered my baby into my arms! Mother was unrepentant; this was the way they bathed babies in her hospital.

Soon, Becky didn't cry as much. I figured that both of us had just been scared of each other, and that we were learning.

Becky and I were out at the base for her six-week checkup. Several times a baby sitter had mentioned that her head was bent over to her shoulder. I figured that all babies' heads wobbled one way or the other; but I mentioned it at the end of the appointment. The doctor, sitting behind his desk, looked at me with that little smile that said this is another of those stupid, young mothers. He reached toward us, putting his hand under Becky's head to lift it off her shoulder. He couldn't. Becky's head was locked in place. I was as shocked as he was. The smile was gone as he came around the desk and grabbed her out of my arms. "Follow me," he said, as he left the office in a run.

"Mrs. Dudley," the doctor said, in between phone calls and reading x-rays, "I'm the pediatrician at this base hospital, but in reality I am just out of school. I haven't passed my boards to be an MD. Most of the doctors here are in the same spot. I think this is a wry neck, where the neck muscle is short or sprained at birth and shortens. But, I don't really know for I have never seen one except as a picture in a medical book. We have an arrangement with a real pediatrician in town who sees cases we don't feel we can handle. I have just called him, and he is expecting you."

"It's her feeding time," I said. "She's hungry."

"Well, your baby will just have to do without. You are to go. Now. The doctor is waiting."

So Becky and I went the ten miles to town to see this new doctor. He sent us to an ophthalmologist who put drops into her baby eyes and examined them. Becky cried because she was hungry. I cried because I was scared and alone. The eye doctor, looking like he wished he could go somewhere else, patted her on the head and gave me a handkerchief. After the exam he said, "I'm pleased to say that all the nerves in Becky's eyes are where and what they are supposed to be."

Back in the pediatrician's office, he tapped on her little knees with a rubber hammer, and hung her in the air, upside down, by holding both of her feet in one hand. As she hung by her heels, her six-week-old baby body curved all to one side. "Mrs. Dudley," the pediatrician said, "I think we have a problem here because it is not just the neck, but all of her left side. I am sending you back to the base where they will check to see if there is pressure on the brain. I have shown the doctors there how to do this, and I'm sure yours will do a good job." Becky had given up, and was asleep. I was too shocked to cry. Back to the base we went.

Ronald had finally found us. He held me in one room while in another they held Becky down and shaved her screaming head so they could put a long needle into her brain to withdraw fluids. This was to see if there was blood and stuff present proving brain damage.

Becky was admitted into the hospital; I was given a cot to sleep on in her room. We settled down for a week's wait while the Air Force lab in San Antonio looked at the fluids removed from her brain. Becky did okay. I learned some more about what life can be, and what courage is all about. Our roommate was a three-year-old who was deformed and mentally disturbed. His mother, on her cot, talked quietly and sanely about their problems.

The week's wait became oddly amusing as the young doctors at our base hospital had, from an expert, a brain damage diagnosis made from the curvature of a baby's body while held by its feet in midair. Up and down the corridors of the hospital, every baby that was brought in was yanked out of mama's arms and held up in the air by its feet. Finally, my doctor came in and said, "Mrs. Dudley, every one we hold up curves one way or the other. Becky's fluid test is back; and it's negative. We don't know what to do, so we are sending you, medical air-evac, down to the big Air Force hospital in San Antonio."

The huge airplane sitting on the runway several days later had its bomb-bay doors open for a stretcher to be loaded. As I walked up with my baby in my arms, the Air Force nurse looked disgusted. "You're it?" she said, not waiting for an answer as she marched away to get her airplane under control.

Becky cried a lot but she was surviving. That was one of the good things about breast-feeding--the process is comforting. I was becoming neurotic, and didn't know how long I was going to get by with not telling anyone that my milk was drying up.

It was 1 a.m. before we got to the hospital in San Antonio. Medical air-evac does not have a schedule. These planes go where they are called. We had ended up in Wichita Falls before we finally arrived in San Antonio. This part of the hospital was an old barracks with no air conditioning; and it was June. Everyone was tired, and miserable, and wet with sweat. It took us over an hour to get through the paper work. Then they sent Becky and me off with a corpsman--who was younger than I was--in charge of getting her into the ward, and me into the base Guest House.

Becky was crying again, making the young corpsman nervous. At the children's ward, I broke down and asked the nurse on duty to give Becky a bottle. The nurse said they had a schedule; she would feed her when it was feeding time. She told me that I could visit at visiting hours, and to go away. I think I went into hysterics. The young corpsman said, "Listen, you have to do something. I have to take this woman to the Guest House, and I can't handle her." So I was allowed to go into another room and try to feed Becky and get her to sleep. Then off we

21

went to the Guest House where, as medical air-evac has priority, I bumped someone's weekend date out of her room at 3 a.m. in the morning.

For the rest of that night, I sobbed into my pillow, blaming Ronald for not being here to fix everything. I felt so alone. Exhaustion the next morning actually helped me let go my neurotic 'feeding-my-baby' issues. I phoned the ward to leave a message that they had a breast baby there that had never been given a bottle. Then I walked down to the cafeteria to try and eat. When I got back, there was an emergency message for me to call the ward. "Get right down here," the nurse said, "the doctor wants to talk to you." I didn't understand bus systems, so I walked the mile to the Children's Neurological Ward of this major Air Force hospital.

The Doctor that met me had dark hair, was of medium height, had a slight twist to his body, and a limp. Deep blue eyes looked me over and turned to Becky, who the nurses had put in a little jump chair by their desk. "Mrs. Dudley," said our doctor, "I want to take you on a tour of my ward. Follow me." I did, and found myself standing in the door of one hospital room watching a young mother feed a bottle to her baby whose head was the size of a basketball. "He won't live to be twenty-one," the doctor said, as his hand on my back firmly moved me on down the hall. There, in a room, was a little boy in a cage. "His mind is completely gone," said the doctor, while he gently closed that room's door. We went through a ward of sadness and horrors--then back to Becky. The doctor smiled and clapped his hands. She cooed and smiled back. He turned to me and said, "Now, don't you ever consider brain damage with this child."

"Since we have a diagnosis of brain damage," the doctor said, taking me into his office, and motioning me to a chair, "we will have to put her through all the tests." I completely broke down. Sobbing like the child I was, I told him that I was having trouble feeding her. "I have five children; and they are all breast babies. We are going to get your milk back. Now don't you worry," he said, pushing a box of Kleenex across the desk. "The rules only allow you to visit at visiting time; but I am ordering you to show up an hour before each of Becky's normal feeding times so you will be there when she wants you. We will work this out together."

Filled with hope, I walked in the heat and dust back to the Guest House. I went to the cafeteria, and bought twenty pints of milk. Stacking them in layers on the little bedside table of my room, I lay down to rest, hoping for a small miracle. R.D. drove in that night. He could stay two days.

It took the hospital five days. The official diagnosis was a wry neck; Becky had sprained it, somehow, at birth. We flew back to Big Spring, and she started physical therapy. The Sergeant that gave it was hairy and bulging with muscle. He was terrified of her. Three times a week we went out to the hospital and our Sergeant put his enormous hands on each side of Becky's head, and slowly moved it from one shoulder to another, gently stretching the neck muscle.

One afternoon as I was leaning against the door watching Sergeant Duff exercising Becky's neck, I heard our doctor calling, "Mrs. Dudley, Mrs. Dudley." I looked up and here he came, white coat tails flapping. In his arms he had a tiny baby with its head stuck down on one shoulder. Running after him was a scared young mother. Becky's wonderful, very young doctor got to me, and holding this baby in his two hands thrust it right into my face. "I want you to diagnose this case for me."

"That's a wry neck," I said with authority.

"Hot Damn! Two of them in one month!" he said, as he turned and charged back down the hall.

DEFCON II

Shreveport Louisiana, 1958
Stephenville, Newfoundland, 1960

I had just begun to get the hang of being a pilot's wife. *About time*, I thought, as orders had arrived for Ernest Harmon, AFB, Stephenville, Newfoundland: our first overseas assignment. When you move a lot, and your husband is gone a lot, and things get tough--in the military your support comes from a sisterhood of women. They give you strength, and they teach you survival skills. Thankfully, I was beginning to realize that a sense of the absurd is not only good for you, it can be learned.

Kevin's birth in Shreveport a few months before we left for our new adventure in Newfoundland was one of those lessons. After being alone when both Becky and Wendy were born in Big Spring, I was determined that this baby would be born in a civilian hospital so Ronald could be there. Just to be sure, R.D. signed up for two back-to-back squadron assignments to Goose Bay, Labrador. Of course, it didn't work. Kevin was three weeks early. This time Daddy wasn't even in the country.

In the middle of the night, I called Ann Bratcher, who had been my neighbor in Big Spring, and, now, lived across the street. "Ann, something is happening," I said. "My bed is wet. Do you suppose my water broke?"

"Oh! God! Hang on. Let me go get my Dr. Spock." In a few minutes she was back on the phone, "We'd better get you to the hospital."

"Ann, I'm not ready! This baby is not due till next month! I don't have anyone to keep the kids."

"I don't either," said Ann. "You call Gloria behind you, and I will get someone to keep mine. Can you get to the door to unlock it?"

"Yes. I'm just scared."

"Don't be. I'll be right there."

An honorary neighborhood midwife association was formed that month with membership belonging to the women who followed me with a mop and helped me get a bag together, the women who stayed with my children, the women who stayed with the children of the women who helped me--and Ann. "I felt so important being a daddy," Ann said. "It's a lot more fun than being a mother. When the doctor came down to tell the father of baby Dudley that he had a boy, I jumped up and down and shouted, 'That's me! I'm the Daddy!' I was really proud when all the other fathers-to-be in the waiting room presented me honorary cigars."

The next morning, the squadron commander's wife, who I had never met, walked into my hospital room with a baby present in her hands. She had in tow a major's wife that I remembered as this woman had hollered at me at the last Wife's Club coffee. I had politely stood up (my father's training) every time the major's wife had walked into a room. She had been furious, and said, "Stop that! You make me feel so old!"

"Do you want me to move into your house," said the squadron commander's wife, "or shall I take your children into mine?" I didn't tell her what that offer meant to me-- something that I still regret, as she, a Christian Scientist, died eight months later of undetected cancer of the uterus. I wouldn't have dreamed of accepting her offer, but the fact that she made it eased my heart. It was a lesson I never forgot.

Ronald flew in from Goose Bay early the next morning.

"Here we go," I said, responding to R.D.'s thumbs up signal. With Becky, Wendy, and new Kevin bedded down in the back of the station wagon, we finally joined our squadron's trek to Harmon. The drive went up the east coast through New Brunswick to Nova Scotia where we boarded the ferry for the eight-hour trip to Port aux Basques, Newfoundland. Then it was north on the only road that existed: one hundred lonely miles of dirt and rock that was listed in the tourist literature as "the last of the great adventure roads." By the time we got on this road, our squadron's trek had littered it with car parts. By the time we got to Stephenville, the frame of our station wagon was warped. We never got the backdoors open again.

At the squadron party to celebrate the safe arrival of all, the winning story of the trip up was about Dunderhead: Major Smith's Newfoundland dog that he brought up from Shreveport. "We were eating lunch at a Howard Johnson's just north of New York City," he said, "with Dunderhead securely tied to the flagpole in front. A cat went by. Dunderhead took off after the cat with the flagpole. He damaged the hoods of ten cars. It was a disaster!"

After the laughter died down, the Colonel rose, "But a joy," he said, with a toast, "to all the friends of Dunderhead."

Our shipment of household goods was another disaster. But as time went by, this disaster became one of my favorite stories. Stephenville, pop. 5000, was on the Atlantic southwest coast of Newfoundland. Specifically, the fishing village sat on a plateau beside Newfoundland's Bay St. George, with the Long Range Mountains to the east. R.D. didn't have the rank to get base housing for the family; and the military said you had to have a place to live before your family could go. So he was really gambling when a week before the deadline he put the children and me on a train to Mom and Dad's in Flat River. At the last moment, a friend came through with one-half of a Quonset hut. That was the reason, R.D. had faced the process of this move by himself.

As soon as we got to Stephenville, R.D. called the squadron. They didn't even give him time to sign in. He was put on alert immediately--in 'the hole' as we learned to call it. The next day, I faced the move into our new home that was in the second row of a group of worn, rectangular, wood buildings that marched across a rocky acre fairly close to the bay.

Our shipment was a mess. Ronald had mentioned, not realizing the consequences, that he hadn't been able to be there with the packers of our household goods. Another comment was that most of his liquor had disappeared. To my distress, the couch arrived with both arms torn off, a game of basketball had obviously been played with the books by pitching them into a box, and our bookcases came in as a bunch of boards with the nails sticking out. Adding to that, the garbage had been carefully packed and shipped.

I actually laughed when we found a large, empty Fab box in our huge washer-dryer combination.

As there wasn't a sticker on a single packing carton, the base inspectors threw up their hands and informed me that they couldn't inspect this shipment or inventory it. They said they would blacklist both packers and movers--then, they left. Edna, the crew engineer's wife who had been in Stephenville a month, showed up and looking horrified said, "Oh! My God! I've never seen anything like this. You have to have help." She found a local electrician to come as the plug to the washer-dryer was one of those big three pronged 220 things. He called a plumber friend. They both stayed from 1 p.m. that afternoon to 11 p.m. that night--fascinated with the mess, and delighted with the Heineken beers that a mildly drunk neighbor kept handing out.

As my piano was carried in--undamaged by some miracle--other of our new neighbors arrived with more beers. Yannie, from the Quonset hut in front of us, said she played. By this time, I'd had two Heinekens, and not being a drinker, I was no longer concerned about my problems. The children were having a great time with all the attention. So, Yannie and I played duets while the rest of the crowd tried to get the washer-dryer to work. The electrician simply cut off the plug, and raw wired the machine into the wall. The growing gang of helpers tried an experimental wash. When they opened the door of our front-loading washer-dryer a wall of suds just stayed there. That was when we realized that the empty box of Fab had been full the day the washer-dryer was shipped. After thirty-two washes, as they tried to get the soap out of the machine, the timer broke. More beers, and the problem solvers got more innovative. They ended up getting a tarp, putting it under the machine and out the kitchen door with people holding up both sides. Then they washed the insides of this front-loading washer-dryer out with a hose.

Suds flowed like lava out of the kitchen and down the steps to the rocky ground outside. Suds mounded into a small mountain that the gathered children threw in the air with joy. It was 11 p.m. when the water from the machine was finally clear of soap. The party broke up, all pleased with the entertaining evening.

I spent some weeks in dread of the expected bills from the electrician and plumber. Not one bill ever showed up. When a Newfoundlander arrived to light our floor furnace in October, he looked at the large machine in the kitchen and the piano in the living room, and with a grin, said, "You're the crazy American who plays duets. That was some party you had!"

Parties are a great way to cope; still, our first one at this new base was a jolt. Normally, when you went into a group of Air Force Officers' wives, you saw a pretty well dressed bunch of women. Harmon had been a Tactical Air Command (TAC) base and some of their pilots had stayed, moved to our Strategic Air Command (SAC). All the women who had been living here looked dowdy; and they were at least twenty pounds overweight.

It didn't take us long to understand the reasons. We slugged around in snow boots nine months of the year; and the town had a Hudson Bay store and one bar. The base commissary (BX) was run by a Georgian from Russia that drank a lot; you could get Rosenthal, Waterford, and Hummels, but forget a washcloth, thread, or any clothes. But, the real problem, we discovered, was the cook at the Officers Club. He was a roaring drunk--and the finest pastry chef ever. At each function, if he was sober, glorious pastries came out by the ton.

A year later, we would sit in sympathy, holding the hands of a young wife sobbing with rage and bitterness over those pastries, our eyes loving the three dresses spread out on her bed. She had been a champion roller skater before her marriage. The Stephenville dowd and bulge had settled on her too. Her rat of a husband flew his plane to New York where he went to a fancy department store. There, with a cocktail in hand and mouth, that man had chosen from the models parading before him the three dresses that lay on the bed--in his wife's size before they were married. As our sole source of anything was from the Sears Catalogue, we all looked in awe and envy at those dresses. God bless her, she did get into one of them before they left the island.

A couple of weeks later, a beautiful black lace dress arrived as a birthday gift from my mother. As I reverently held it up before me, I was astonished, stunned, and then accepting. My beautiful dress was a petite size 16. Since I had stood 5'8" from the 6th grade and wore a size 12, I wondered what my mother saw when she looked at me. Ah well, I thought as I regretfully put down my dress, this is what makes our personalities, and I kind of like mine--so it's okay. Besides, there would be someone on this island who would be ecstatic to get this as an early Christmas gift.

Around the middle of November that first year, I began to really bitch about Newfoundland: How could we be this far north and not have snow? Where was our white Christmas?

It started really snowing about the middle of December. It quit on the 10th of March--two hundred and seventy-three inches and not one flake melted. It came down in curtains; it came down like popcorn balls; it snowed in horizontal sheets. The snow stopped when the ice pack came into the bay between Nova Scotia and our island. The base had snow equipment, but the fishing village had a truck and shovels. We lived in tunnels of white with ribbons of blue sky above us. We left our Quonsets off porches, or through windows. It was beautiful! When we first arrived in Stephenville, we laughed at some of the square wood houses painted pink, green, blue, or a combination. In all that white, those houses became flowers in the snow.

Our military family would drive out on that snow the next March so R. D. could spend three months in San Antonio upgrading to aircraft commander in KC 97s. It was an extraordinary journey. That road of dirt and rock had become a wide swath of white lined with dark green conifers. The air was full of ice crystals that in the early morning light shimmered in layers of pale pink and green like banks of fairy fog. When we got to Port aux Basque, that huge ferry, broad of beam and round of bottom, carried six cars and fifteen people. As the ferry was drawing about two inches of water and bobbed like a cork, my stomach was pretty well panicked, and therefore grateful, when we hit the pack ice just outside the harbor.

There, a strange trip began that would take twenty-four hours instead of the normal eight. The old boat backed up, revved its motors, and charged the ice--literally riding up on it. Then a great cracking would start, and the ice would break--the boat falling through to the water. Backing up, motors revving, she would charge the ice again. We repeated this process all the way across.

I will never forget that ice. We hung onto the railing, riding that strange chariot, mesmerized by the pack ice spotted with icebergs. Most of that ice that is deep down below the water makes you think of sapphires. The ice bergs glowed from inside with the same awesome blue. *The Titanic*, I thought, *went down because of ice like this.* On our ferry's very next trip from Port aux Basques to Nova Scotia, it got stuck in that pack ice for two weeks, a helicopter had to drop supplies. They got their pictures in Life Magazine.

Newfoundland was constantly an adventure. It wasn't unusual to get caught at the base for several days when we had a "whiteout." Your children would be taken from school and put in base homes. It was not rare to end up camping out at the Officers Club having to break into the commissary to get the things needed for a couple of days stay. Whiteouts were serious business. You could lose your car by just stepping away from it. That old saying "you couldn't see the hand in front of your face" was a dangerous reality.

My children were never a concern if I got stuck on base in a whiteout as my baby sitter Mary was fifteen and the oldest of fourteen children. She was better at handling a house and kids than I would ever be. Stephenville had very large families; eighteen was an average number. A family living up the street from us had twenty-four living children, and one living mother. The women were all lovely when they were young; they lost their teeth by the time they were twenty-five; and the only thing that stopped the pregnancies was age, or death.

An influx of young women, with their husband's right out of flight school, came at the end of our two-year tour. They brought with them birth control pills and tranquilizers--both new to us, as at that time the military didn't dispense either one. When they started arriving, the older wives deliberately gathered up the newcomers, including them into every dinner, bridge game, and party. I had stopped by a friend's house after an afternoon of bridge to tell her all the gossip. "Kathy," I said, "you won't believe these new kids and their panic about running out of their birth control pills. One of the husbands is going to take a plane to the states and load up. Every new wife I have met is taking these tranquillizer things to stay calm so they can cope if they run out their pills."

The Newfoundland woman, of indeterminate age, in the small kitchen with us was doing Kathy's ironing. Kathy had noticed when I grimaced and looked away because the woman's legs were horrifying great ridges of purple veins. "Oh Mary, I hope we haven't upset you with our conversation about birth control pills," Kathy said. "Sue, Mary has eighteen children."

We both got a long look from tired eyes. "If I had known of anything that could have helped me," Mary said, "I would have used it." The kitchen sank into frustrated silence. Feeling depressed, I got up and left.

The Royal Canadian Mounted Police, law on the spot in Stephenville, had come by our Quonsets when we were new to tell us that handing a piece of information about birth control to a Newfoundlander was illegal and we could be arrested (this was 1960 through 1962). They also told us that shooting anyone for any reason was murder, even if they were crawling into your house with a knife in hand.

We didn't blame the young, handsome, and very big Mounties for Canada's laws, although we were both furious and sad over the "no information about birth control" one. Still, we liked their version of justice. Late one night as Ronald and I were sitting on the steps watching a lavender and green aurora borealis play over the snow, the Mounties stopped a car on our street. One casually leaned against the passenger door. The other pulled the driver out with one hand and sat him on the trunk of the car. After a couple of hard slaps, we heard our Mountie say, "I want you to understand that this will be the last time you ever hit your wife in public. What you do in your own home is yours, but if you ever do what you did this evening, it's mine."

On the whole, the military was amused, and they honored the Mounties' idea of fairness. When the GIs started a fight in Stephenville's only bar and beat up a Mountie, he picked himself up, went to the Mountie barracks and turned them all out. Those Mounties went back to the bar and cleaned house. Then they stacked the GIs up outside, and called the MPs to come get them. No charges or complaints--that was it.

In Stephenville, the local men were small and dark, worked as little as possible, and had bad backs. They caught lobsters. At the base, we could get a carton of cigarettes for ninety-nine cents; then, we could trade the carton for one dozen lobsters. The lobsterman would take you out in a boat to the pens and let you pick your own. Some were huge; I never cooked less than a dozen lobsters. It was such fun to have a military friend show up from the states and feed him the dinner of his dreams.

Our social lives revolved around the only place we had: the Officers Club. You could meet your husband there when he was on alert, for the crews were allowed to go; they just could not drink alcohol. We had three nights at that club that would become famous. The party given for the new captains of 1961 that included Ronald was just flat wonderful. Johnny Cash and his group had come to Newfoundland to hunt moose. The weather was foul and they all caught colds. Somehow they ended up in Stephenville and the Officers Club got them for that night. They played and sang and then partied with us until the wee hours of the morning. Johnny had trouble staying on key in good times. He didn't even try that night and no one cared.

Then the Australians arrived. They got their flying time once a year instead of each month like our Air Force did. They would take off and go around the world. This plane had stopped in England to load up with teachers for their schools. It broke down, and they were at Harmon for a week waiting for an engine to arrive. Since most of these teachers were women, our bachelors were ecstatic. The Australians taught us a new game: Dead Bug. A person walking into the bar would call out "Dead Bug." Then all the crazy people sitting at the bar would fall off on their backs, hands and feet in the air. Last one down had to buy a round for the bar. No one got hurt, which was amazing, but the squadron commander stopped it after the Australians left.

The worse-for-drink that I ever saw a whole Officers Club get was toward the end of our two years; it was an Air Force gesture of sympathy and solidarity with one of their fellow pilots. This Captain, obviously in shock, walked into the Club about 8 p.m. He had gotten his orders. He was going to Churchill, Canada--north from Newfoundland. A quiet, commiserating group drank to him and bought drinks for him, doing in that moment the best they could do.

Hardship overseas melds a squadron into a family, as you have no one else. Harmon qualified, and the tougher it got the closer we got. This was the nuclear war era, and we all listened to Moscow Molly on Grundig radios from that crazy BX. One night she said, "Hello Harmon, AFB in Newfoundland. You really ought to do something about that light that is out on your tower." When they checked, she was right. We stomped around for weeks saying, "Oh! Shit!" After all, this was a SAC base; these were the tankers that would refuel the B-52 Bombers if they had to go to Russia.

Ronald kept reminding me after we got to Harmon that he was getting extra pay because the military considered this a hardship assignment. It was worse than that. We didn't have enough crews. In the Air Force, pilots were supposed to have a set number of hours of rest between flights. Our guys were not getting them.

One month R.D. had twenty-three hours to spend off alert. We stuffed those precious hours. The air was clear that day so we took the kids ice-skating. Our favorite pond was covered with snow, again. A covey of young Stephenville potential hockey players edged it looking disgusted, as they wanted to play. Between us, we got it cleared. Afterward, when we lost Wendell in a big snowdrift, our new team-mates helped to dig him out. We made love. We laughed with friends. Every minute was precious and intense.

A special buddy of ours, Petey, Robert Peterson, had had it, which was a statement in itself as Petey was an easygoing squadron character. When we were in Shreveport, Petey was driving home late one night from the Officers Club, and a police car in front of him was going too slow over the bridge. He rammed it, and signaled with his arm out the window for them to speed up. When they didn't, he rammed it again, and signaled with more energy. The police turned on their lights and pulled Petey over.

They ordered him to get out of the car. "Are you crazy," said Petey to the officer, "I'm too drunk to stand up." One of the policemen drove Petey's car, and the other drove Petey home. They took him to Charlene and told her to make him behave.

Now, at Harmon, Petey was so tired of the tough schedule that he told the flight surgeon he saw spots. Petey had been seeing spots for years (they turned out to be loose cells in the eye) and not wanting to lose flight status had kept his mouth shut. At this time, he didn't care if he lost flight status. He had had it.

Ronald and Petey had both applied for college. R.D. had been trying to get the military to let him finish his degree for years. It finally came through. Every Friday the guys weren't on alert, we celebrated: Ronald and I, Petey and Charlene. We made such grand plans. The boys, deciding on the University of Colorado, bought us all hand-knit Norwegian ski sweaters that showed up in our crazy BX. Then, planning a little subtle bribery, they took a plane full of liquor to the States. They let guys hitch a ride as long as they gave the pilots their liquor allowance. Later, R.D. said bitterly, that the major in charge of assignments must have been the only teetotaler in the military. We ended up at Oklahoma State University, and Petey and Charlene went to the University of Pittsburgh.

Our orders for college were here! The excitement was beyond hysteria! We were going back to the States--home! The movers had come; our goodbye parties were this week.

Then, on October 20th, 1962, everything was put on hold. SAC slammed its doors shut.

October 22, President Kennedy told the world about the missiles in Cuba. That day, SAC went into Defense Condition Three (DEFCON III) that consisted of a massive airborne alert of the B-52 bombers. All the pilots of the tankers were pulled on alert. Later that day, SAC went into DEFCON II. SAC had never been in that alert before. It meant that B-52s were loaded with nuclear bombs and a number of them kept in the air at all times. To our squadron, it meant that if the horn blew, they were going to nuclear war. Their mission would be refueling the B-52s on their way to Russia with all the fuel our planes had. Our crews were not coming back. They would be ditching in the ocean. The Military ordered the women and children onto the base. We were issued forms from the US Government that said anyone that helped us get back to the States would be reimbursed.

All KC 97s were ordered to Harmon. There were a couple of squadrons in the states; they came. As the KC 97s were being slowly replaced by the new KC 135s, this order included an occasional 97 that had been left at some base. We had stories on stories. Some commander would say: "Has anyone here ever flown a 97? Have you ever seen one?" And up they came. One crew was made up of a pilot that had been a co-pilot once, his copilot had never been in a 97, his engineer had never seen one, and his boom operator had a broken arm.

The night that they all came in, Harmon had one of the worst storms of our two years. That is saying something for the winds were fierce on this island. There were ropes on the runways for sometimes the guys had to crawl to the planes. At one end of the Harmon runways you had the mountains, at the other end the bay. Petey commanded the tower that night. He said the tower was swaying so bad that they should have evacuated it; instead they sat braced on the floor. A lot of what we had seen in these two years we thought of as a military farce. Right now, we were as close to the real thing as I hope we ever get, with craziness everywhere, and everything worked like it was supposed to. It was a miracle.

All the families that lived off base were pulled on. If someone was pregnant in the apartments, a woman was chosen to go to the hospital and get a quick course on birthing. The sisterhood worked in quiet efficiency. Not one woman cried or fell apart. We filled tubs with water and did what we could think of to do, except no one knew, for no one had been here before. The kids and I were sent on base to Bonnie Williams. She didn't have children, just a Persian cat. When I got there with Becky, Wendy, and Kevin --my little troupers loaded down with blankets, toys, and food--I was beginning to lose my ability to be brave. We found Bonnie and Pookey in her basement with three cases of cat food and two cases of scotch. "That's it," Bonnie said, "the important things are here." For some reason it struck me as funny and I settled down.

The day the ships met at sea, we were all at the Officers Club glued to the radio waiting for the world's fate, and ours, to be decided. That evening a dirty, tired Major walked into the Club looking completely phased out. The poor man had been on leave when his squadron was sent to Harmon. He had hopped planes, hitched rides, and caught a boat to Corner Brook, fifty miles north of Stephenville on that "last of the great adventure roads." He had just arrived after a three-hour ride on the island bus. Everyone in the club saluted him in both amusement and awe.

While the ships sat there and looked at each other, the Dudleys and the Petersons began to fret about those college assignments. On October 28th, the Russian Premier Nikita S.

Khrushchev ordered the Russian supply ships away from Cuba, and the missiles dismantled. We began to breathe again, although SAC did not return to DEFCON III until November 15th.

The squadron commander took Ronald off alert and told him that if things stayed quiet, we could leave. Petey, as a non-flying officer, wasn't on alert and they snuck out the next day.

SAC was still in DEFCON II, but we were living in the guesthouse hoping to get a final okay to go. That morning, the whole family was getting breakfast at the cafeteria on the flight line. Trays in hands, we were facing the wall of glass that looked out on the planes--at that instant, a big explosion rattled the windows. The horn went off. We just stood there in shock! In a moment, a truck went by the windows in front of us dropping soldiers with carbines in their hands--drop, drop, drop, like clockwork right in front of us. We could see off to our right flames roaring up into the sky. Ronald ran for a phone! The horn continued to blare. Trucks and planes started to move. The world went crazy!

The pilots and crews on alert only heard that horn. This was it! They ran for war! Heads were split open on doors. Pants were not pulled up from the pot. Shoes weren't on. They simply ran for the planes.

What they did was move them.

A sergeant had been checking the small concrete sheds that housed all the wiring and mechanical stuff for refueling the planes on the flight lines. He smelled gas in one and hit the fan switch. It shorted and blew the house up and him across the fight line. The base could only think of those hundreds of planes parked wing tip to wing tip on that concrete that had under it the gas lines. Command was afraid all of it would explode so they blew the alert horn--to move those planes. It worked! We were all both amazed and proud! There were a couple of trucks wrecked, our sergeant was deaf for a week, and a lot of silly stories accrued. Not one plane was damaged.

The next day the commander called and said, "I'll cover for you. Tomorrow, just go." That evening, the Colonel and his wife arrived at our room in the Guesthouse. In the dark, because of the DEFCON II alert, sitting on the floor with candles lit, they unpacked a basket with wine and hors d'oeuvres. We partied, high on stories and silliness, just the four of us in the best tradition of making do and saying a squadron goodbye.

Early the next day we left--the children asleep in the back of a station wagon whose doors would not open. We were on the road again, driving away from Stephenville. "We're on another adventure," I said. "I'm glad it's snowing."

"Yes," said R. D. with a smile at me, "I'm glad too."

WENDY

Stillwater, Oklahoma, 1962
Hampton, Virginia, 1964

When he was five years old, Wendell severed the thumb to his right hand in an accident in our home. He was showing his sister how a jet airplane goes by putting a plastic bullet into the outlet pipe of our combination washer-dryer while it was drying. To get his hand into the fan blades, Wendell had to put his arm in the pipe all the way to his shoulder--we measured.

Happy, bombastic Wendy, with his carrot red hair and big, round, brown eyes, was the middle child and the most precocious of our three children. The ice cream truck man let Wendy ride the neighborhood with him and gave him ice cream bars. The workmen building new houses around us in Stillwater had lumber, nails, and a hammer off to the side of their job for Wendell. When we stopped at traffic lights in town, women on the sidewalk were drawn up to the car windows smiling in response to Wendy's glowing personality and loud, happy "Hey" and "Hellos."

In the bathroom, the night Wendell changed his life, I tried to stop the blood flowing from what was left of the right hand of my darling five-year-old child. Seeing the white bones protruding where the thumb used to be, I felt myself graying out with nausea and hysteria. "No!" The order slammed through my brain. From my childhood, my mother commanded: "You WILL DO what you have to do. You WILL NOT throw up, faint, cry, or to let go in any way." So with as much calm as I could fabricate, I did what I had to do.

At the emergency room of the hospital they refused to give Wendell anything for the pain without a doctor's request. They refused to call a doctor until we said who we wanted. We were a military family, just arrived as Ronald was to finish his engineering degree at Oklahoma State University. We didn't have a doctor. I thought R.D. was going to hit someone. Then, out of the shocked recesses of my mind came the name of the man who had done Becky's first grade school exam. Immediately, this doctor ordered morphine and called the foremost hand surgeon in the Midwest. They gave us Wendell's thumb on ice, and we raced for Mercy Hospital in Oklahoma City.

The hours of surgery were spent in hope and trying to make sense of what had happened. Wendell would have had to take the outlet hose's metal clamps off the large pipe that came out of the dryer to get his arm into the machine. The dryer was drying. The metal pipe must have been hot. Children normally stay away from hot; I never would understand it.

I was sick and dull with fear and could only take my heart to Wendy's room, where I often went when I felt in need--just to sit on the floor by his bed. That's where I was in my mind when the doctor came to tell us that they could not reattach Wendell's thumb, but he had been able to save the index finger. Still not allowed to cry, I went into a place where I could endure. Ronald came very close to fainting with the news. Later that day, R.D left because he had to go back to college. I stayed.

For three days tears continuously streamed down my face as I talked, ate, and apologized. "Please excuse me," I said, to doctors, nurses, and strangers, "I'm sorry. They won't stop."

The children's ward at Mercy Hospital allowed the adults complete access. We could sleep anywhere we could find, in a chair or on a coffee table. The regulars got to be friends as we spent the nights together in the lounge. I talked a lot with an Otoe Indian grandmother whose granddaughter had leukemia. The Otoes were members of the Pawnee Indian Nation. Her stories of the Oklahoma Indian life were different than I expected. All her children had a college education; in Oklahoma, it was free to them. In Oklahoma, the Indian children born before 1905 were given ten acres of land, normally out in nowhere. "If they kept it," she said, with a smug look, "they usually ended up with oil wells." We both latched onto another of our fellow storytellers, a traveling salesman whose daughter had cancer. He could tell jokes all night. I laughed as those tears continued to stream down my face.

After a week in Mercy Hospital, Wendy and I were on our way home when, out in the middle of nowhere, the car had a flat tire. I could see one lonely house on top of a hill. Walking over fields and climbing over fences, we headed for that sign of humanity. There, an Indian family gave us a drink of water, access to a phone, and advice on who to call. Back at the car, we waited. The man arrived and found the spare tire flat. Wendy and I rode in an old truck into a dusty barren town to wait in the heat as he fixed the tire. A couple of hours after the flat, we were on the road again.

When we finally got home, my mother and father, who had been found by Texas Rangers in Big Bend National Park, were fixing supper. I decided to help by making the iced tea, and stupidly poured the boiling liquid into my Waterford pitcher. The sound of the cracking crystal actually moved through my body. For a strange moment, I felt like that ice as our boat broke through it on the trip back from Newfoundland. Excusing myself, I went into my bedroom and on my bed, pulling my pillow to my heart—finally, finally, I broke down and sobbed.

Later that summer the family accepted an invitation from my Oto friend to go to the Pawnee Powwow in Ponca City. The powwow took place in the center of a dusty high school football field. A roaring fire was going in the middle while off to one side the Indian drummers, in leather with lots of beads and feathers, provided a blood-pounding beat. We were only allowed to watch, and sat on bare wood bleachers at one side of the field. Down on the field, to our left, were rows of wood benches for the participants. Some Otos were glorious in full Indian dress with lots of eagle feathers; some were in blue jeans--all wore moccasins for the dancing. I was fascinated with one lady, in a dress, who had a full-length mink coat beside her on the bench. Every time she joined the dancers, she would drag that mink coat behind her in the dust around and around the fire.

That July in Oklahoma was hot, hot, hot. As we sat in the bleachers, R.D., in shorts, kept yelping and jumping. He had lots of curly hair on his legs, and the Indian children were getting souvenirs by sneaking behind and below the benches and yanking his curls out. By the time we left, R.D. had bald spots on both legs.

Summer passed, and Wendy entered first grade with a right hand that could only work like a pincer; it could not hold a pencil. He had a bad time trying to use his left hand. Every teacher, and his mother, hollered at him because his school papers would have a mark here, a mark there, and then be erased all the way through. No one understood what was going on. It would be several years before doctors did the operations at UCLA separating the right and left brains that might have given us some information on the difficulties: his brain was jamming. Wendy was coping, alone, as his mind worked through this traumatically forced transfer from his right hand to his left hand.

Wendy's teacher--a Ph.D. paid by the town and the University, who taught a teaching classroom with a one-way mirror in the back--called me in for a conference. "Mrs. Dudley," she said, "Wendell tests way above the work he is doing. I'm concerned."

"Maybe it has something to do with his right hand problem."

"What do you mean, right hand problem?" she said.

"He is right handed and can just use his fingers to 'pince' without that thumb."

"He doesn't have a thumb on his right hand?" she said, looking distraught. "Oh! My God! I didn't know."

"Wendell has been so good about everything that he often seems to not have a problem," I said. "If you ask him he will show you, and explain it to you. We have been told to leave him alone and let him make the change to his left hand."

"Mrs. Dudley, there is no excuse for me not knowing about Wendell, but I have eleven very disruptive boys in my class this year, and the only thing I can do is try to keep control. I'm sorry."

I was sorry too. The stories about Wendy before the accident were funny examples of a child making sense of his world. Once when we were going to a nursery in east Stillwater to get some plants for our yard, Becky, who was in first grade, became very quiet and said, "Momma, we're in the colored part of town."

Wendy, never to be left out or ignored, with carrot hair standing on end, and huge brown eyes glowing, said, "Yeh! Colored houses! Colored trees! Colored flowers!"

He was such a treat. In Oklahoma the young ladies had added Cleopatra make-up to their beehive hairdos. One day close to Halloween, I had to take Wendy to the beauty shop with me. He, fully engaged with this exotic season, went rigid when we walked into the shop, staring at the young receptionist with her beehive hair-do and very, very, heavily made up face. To my horror, Wendell, at the top of his voice, pointing his finger at her, and brimming with excitement, said, "Mommy, I want a Halloween just like that one!"

Wendell's personality began to change in the year after the accident. He became tense and unhappy. We desperately wanted to get some help and began to push the military for a transplant. Our request was accepted. The Air Force required that we go to their big new hospital in San Antonio. An operation was scheduled, and off we went.

Ronald drove us to Texas, but would catch a plane back that night for he was in finals. When we arrived, the nurse insisted that we sign a pre-operation form that exempted the doctor, and the military, from everything in the operation scheduled for the next morning. R.D. said I would have to sign it, for he was leaving; I was the one who would be responsible. When I read it, I wouldn't sign. "We haven't even talked to the doctor," I said. "I can't sign this."

As the hours passed the nurse came back. "Mrs. Dudley, you have to sign this, or we will cancel your son's operation."

"You haven't taken any X-rays; I can't sign this," I said, shaking and sick to my stomach."

And, again, and again, "Mrs. Dudley, you have to sign this form."

"I can't until I see a doctor," I said, and ran for the bathroom where I threw up.

At 7 p.m., a harried young doctor came charging into the room, nodding at us, yelling for the nurse, demanding the records. Then, in disgust, he said, "I can't do this operation; I don't have x-rays." Poor man, I collapsed on his shoulder in tears and relief. "That's it," he said. "We need to calm you down. We'll cancel tomorrow morning and do the operation after we talk."

"You can transplant the big toe, or the ring finger," he said, as he sat us down in his office, "or split the hand at the index finger and turn it for a thumb. I'm a plastic surgeon, and I am going to turn the index finger." He arraigned for me to consult with an orthopedic surgeon who had done this particular operation. The next day was to be filled with x-rays and tests. I would see the orthopedic surgeon on the second day, and the operation was scheduled for the third. At 9 p.m., he walked us out to the parking lot. Ronald left to catch a plane back to Oklahoma; and, I found my way to the same base Guest House that I had used when Becky was in the old hospital.

The orthopedic surgeon was very nice and explained things carefully to me. Then he said, "I have some pictures of a hand that I did last year. She severed her thumb while water skiing when the rope tangled around it."

The pictures were horrible. I tried not to look as shocked as I was. Her hand, in its new configuration, seemed to have worms instead of fingers. Years later in Okinawa, I would lay my bridge cards on the table and reach for the hand of the woman across from me. "You lost your thumb in a skiing accident," I would say to her in response to her surprise. "I have a story to tell you…"

But, on this day I just got myself out of the office, and nearly hysterical, called R.D. He said, "I've had it. I'm in finals. I can't do this. Just come home."

In two hours, I had Wendell out of the hospital. We spent a memorable night sleeping together in the Guest House. I had a bladder infection and went to the bathroom thirteen times; and Wendy wet the bed and me. At 5 a.m. I gave up, and we left San Antonio for Stillwater. Our trip home was longer and more adventurous than the trip down. There are two roads north out of San Antonio. I took the wrong one.

Orders had arrived, and we were going to TAC Headquarters, Hampton, Virginia, just a five hour drive from Washington, D.C. Immediately on getting them, we inquired at Walter Reed about a transplant, and were accepted.

For weeks, I would make that drive from Hampton and an appointment at Walter Reed in one day. Wendell was a special patient; we had a note from Dr. Butler that he was to be called when we came in. This was the middle of the Vietnam War, and hand operations were a big part of Dr. Butler's schedule. But, Dr. Butler had never done one on a child; and he was excited.

The best hand surgeon in the world, from Boston, was helping Butler. They decided to do a fourth-finger transplant. There would be three operations. The first would take the fourth-finger through the hand and place it where the thumb used to be. They would remove all bones and signs of the fourth-finger making the third finger and little finger sit together as if that were normal. Wendell would end up with the ring finger gone, and a long, narrow white scar between the third and little fingers. The second operation would cut off the end joint of the fourth-finger new thumb, and transplant the fingernail onto the second joint to make it look more like a thumb. The third operation was for cosmetic effect, and would pad the new thumb. "What we have found out," said Dr. Butler, "is that our operations can be a success. But, if the patient doesn't like the way it looks, puts his hand in his pocket and doesn't use it--we've really failed."

One afternoon at Walter Reed, I waited in an office with another Air Force mother whose son had been there for a year. She had an apartment for they were based in Idaho. We liked each other. She was one of the reasons that I left later than usual that day and hit the beltway around D.C. in going home traffic. It was horrible! Cars and trucks poured around me. I was scared enough to wonder if we were going to get home alive. Then the radio traffic guy started rerouting cars as he told us that traffic was piling up for miles in all directions around a certain bridge that had had a wreck on it. After a little while, a bland radio voice came on and said, "Ladies and Gentlemen, anyone planning to cross this bridge just sit back, put your feet up and light another cigarette. There has been a wreck in the other lanes of the bridge. The only way off this bridge is to jump." Laughing, because I wasn't in that mess, I relaxed and drove on home.

The drives to D.C. were starting to worry me as I did not have a Virginia driver's license; mine was from Florida (A lot of the military, even if you had not been based there, had a FL driver license.) Wendy and I were to go to Walter Reed the next day to stay. I was very stressed out as I still had not found a place to live for the month my son would be in the hospital. Getting my driver's license, I decided, might help my nerves. The officer giving the driver's tests that day must have been having a bad time. When my tires touched the paint on the concrete parking lot that marked a parallel parking place, he exploded. He tore up my paperwork, threw it on the ground, shouting at me to come back some other day, and stomped away. I was so upset and crying so hard, that I had to stop on the way home to get some control.

That evening the phone rang. A woman's voice said, "Is this the Dudley family that has a child coming to Walter Reed?"

"Yes it is."

"Sue?"

"Yes."

"This is Joy. I have been calling all the Dudleys in the phone book trying to locate you. We've been transferred to Hampton. I wanted to find out if you would like to stay in my Silver Springs apartment with me while Wendell is in Walter Reed?"

There are angels, I thought with enormous relief as I put down the phone. I would think that again one night as I sat in that shabby, musty smelling apartment house with Joy and another young military wife who had lived there for several months. This young woman, an orphan, had lost her whole family. Her husband had been brought home from Vietnam when their only child died; then they found out he had cancer. That evening her husband had died. Joy held her as I sat with them. We all cried.

Walter Reed was full of young men, and some young women, who had been injured in Vietnam. It was a city in itself. Several hospitals were connected through underground tunnels. This night, I was pushing Wendy in his wheelchair to a movie. I had noticed one of the many patients in our tunnel, wondering about him. I couldn't guess his age. He was young, and yet old; and, he walked funny. The young-old man came over and insisted that since he was also going to the movie, he push Wendy. We struck up a conversation. "How long have you been here?"

"At Walter Reed? Two years," he said.

"What happened?" I said, Wendy and I both looking at him with big eyes.

"I landed a helicopter upside-down in Vietnam," he said, with a wry grin as he glanced at us, "and broke every bone in my body."

Our new friend parked Wendy, and me, in a wheel chair section in the back, and left to join some of his buddies. The theater was full. Most of them young men, or what was left of them, in pajamas and wheel chairs.

The movie was a kick! It was Elvis Presley in long robes crawling under tents and singing. To me it was an unexpected gift, as the audience, my military family, started talking back to Elvis, and had a great time razzing the other actors on the screen. We all laughed and laughed. It was a very special evening.

Okinawa Here We Come!

Hampton, Virginia, 1964
Englewood, Florida, 1965

"I will never put down wall-to-wall carpeting again," I said, adding a few of my new swear words and throwing something I didn't like very much on the floor. Our guaranteed four-year assignment had ended in nine months; Ronald had orders. He was to fly, mostly in Vietnam, C-130s, the big transport planes based in Naha AB, Okinawa. My job was to sell the house, put the bulk of our stuff in storage, and move the rest, with the children and me, to a trailer park in Florida--to wait. R.D., a Captain, did not have enough rank to get us on base, and his job was to find something for us to live in. Wendell's third operation on his new thumb would be scheduled from Florida.

Right now, I was sick. Ronald was out of town, and I was out of my head. The children survived somehow. I can remember crawling up the stairs to my bed. "I look funny, my ear is swollen," I said in all seriousness to my reflection in the bathroom mirror, "what is this rash on my face?" I could tell I had a fever.

R.D. came home and took me out to the base hospital. The rash had disappeared so they thought I had the flu. He left. When I didn't get any better, I decided that it was psychosomatic, pure guilt – the cause: I was still driving without a Virginia driver's license. So running 102 degrees of fever, I got out of bed and went to take the driver's test. This time I passed it. Back in my bed, with hands folded over my breasts, I waited, expecting to get well. It didn't work.

Ronald, home again, took me back to the hospital. "You," the doctor said when I told him about the rash, "must have the German measles." I clearly remember the smug pleasure I felt as we left that office. The German measles had just been given to the whole driver's license department by me; it felt wonderful! R.D. left, again. The next time he came home, there was a swelling on the back of my head the size of a baseball. That was the last straw; he took me out to the fight surgeon's office where the pilots went. These doctors were fascinated--several of them "Oh'ed" and "Ah'ed" over my lump. After the whole story was told, they had no idea what was going on except that the swelling was a lymph gland. So they gave me every test they could think of. All of them came out fine except the throat swab; to everyone's surprise, I cultured beta strep.

The children started getting sick. I would grab them by the shoulders and chin, and say, "Stick out your tongue and say Aww." White spots in their throats, and out to the base hospital we would go. When R.D. got strep, the doctors were exasperated, and cultured the whole family, even the dog. I was fine, I thought, no sore throat, just a little tired. But, I was the one that cultured beta strep. "You're a 'carrier,'" said the doctor, with accusation in his eyes. For a long time I kept a note in my purse that allowed me to walk into any Air Force lab and get a culture done--which I would do if I started feeling tired and found a low grade fever. Every time, it was beta strep.

We took our craziness with us to Englewood, Fl. Ronald was in Montgomery, AL training in C-130s. The dog, the kids and I were in a trailer park with Mom and Dad. They, in a one-bedroom, kept Becky and Wendell. Kevin, Gretchen, our schnauzer, and I lived in their 16 ft. travel trailer. This particular day I was at MacDill AFB to set up medical air evac for Wendell's last operation. While I was there, I went to see about our shipment--the military had lost it. I looked sternly at the Sergeant who was trying to explain. "Mrs. Dudley," he said, "we can't find the driver. He just quit and unloaded your stuff, somewhere. We are inventorying every warehouse on the whole southeast coast. We will find it."

My problems were superficial. The young woman at the next desk was explaining that her husband had been killed in Vietnam, and she was being hassled with scary phone calls. Our eyes met, and I smiled and lifted my hand to her sending a hug across the room. This was a period of time in our U.S. history that if you were a military dependent you needed to be close to a base so your military family could put their arms around you.

The military air evac Wendell and I got on later that month was full of people, some sick, a lot with bad hearts. The plane was flying low and unpressurized because they couldn't get the bomb-bay doors shut. We were having a really rough ride. I was feeling very sorry for everyone else until Wendy got airsick and threw up on me. This was not good for they took our luggage when we got on at MacDill and told us we would get it back at Walter Reed. At one stop several young people in blue pajamas, and robes, and face masks got on. They had T.B. I began to pray that we wouldn't catch something. After several days plane hopping all over the east coast, I wanted clean clothes. We spent nights in some base hospital ward somewhere. They would kindly let me have blue pajamas to wear. I would wash out my underwear with a bar of soap in the bathroom sink, and put them on damp the next day. A strap had broken on my sandals, and I had to tie it with string. We may not have been sick people when we got on that plane, but we sure looked like we needed help by this time. Because air-evac goes when called, they wouldn't let me leave the hospital ward to get to a base exchange for anything. On the fifth day we landed at Schenectady, N.Y., and that evening at Andrews AFB, Washington, D.C.

A bus was waiting on the flight line to carry us to Walter Reed. The driver stood before his numb passengers, and said, "Ladies and Gentlemen, we are going to stay here beside the flight line for several hours. A Star Flight is bringing wounded in directly from Vietnam. We will be here until this air plane lands in case they need us. I know you want to get on to Walter Reed, and I apologize. But, everybody waits on these planes. Even Generals are scrubbed and waiting at Walter Reed right now. Our guys come first." You didn't get one word of complaint out of us. We understood.

It was 1 a.m. and raining when the bus pulled into Walter Reed. Just as we got down the steps, I looked up and framed in the light of the hospital doorway stood Ronald. I was stunned. *A miracle*, I thought. "Where in the hell have you been?" he said. "Medical air evac lost you. Doctor Butler has been beside himself. Wendell's operation was supposed to have been yesterday." Wendy was fortunate as he was the only patient on that bus that had a room at Walter Reed. They put everyone else back on the bus, and took them to the Guest House at Andrews AFB. I felt really blessed; I got a bath, clean clothes--and R.D.

It was two days before Christmas. The children, dog, and I were staying in the 24-foot trailer. Mom and Dad had decided they preferred to be by themselves in the little one. The children were in bed, and I was sobbing on the couch--so alone and sad. It had been months as Ronald was having a house built. We weren't scheduled to go to Okinawa until Jan 21st. As our surprise Christmas present, R.D. walked in the door. He had flown a plane from Naha to South Carolina for maintenance; it wouldn't be ready to go back until Jan. 10th. We filled every day. It was a glorious time!

Okinawa, here we come. The found 'stuff' was shipped, even the dog. I was still sane and standing in the Seattle Airport waiting for a Northwest Orient Flight that would take us through Fairbanks, Alaska to Tokyo. The children were jumping around like fleas. After watching a young woman with a baby sitting on some luggage and looking very upset, I walked over and said, "Hi, my name is Sue. Are you by any chance going to Okinawa?" She threw her arms around me and began to sob on my shoulder. As I held her, the story tumbled out. *Every time I believe I'm at my limit,* I thought, as I listened through her hiccups and sobs, *I am humbled.*

Sarah was an orphan. She had married a young Marine who was sent to Okinawa. Sarah, with baby in arms, had been put on her very first airplane by her father-in-law in Maine. "Honey," he said, "don't be afraid; people will help you." In the Chicago airport, she sat on her luggage and cried. No one helped. I was the first person to talk to her.

That Northwest Orient flight was filled with a lot of military of all ranks going to Okinawa through Japan: Air Force, Navy, Army, and Marines. On that trip, men going to war played with our children. Young Marines changed diapers and bottle-fed the baby. My three played with battle ribbons and threw them in the air. The Air Force Colonel, a dentist, pinned his medals on Wendy and Kevin. It was a trip to remember forever, and another view of that military family that I will always be so proud of.

By the time we landed in Tokyo, the Colonel had organized the hodge-podge of military into a group; and he included us. We were to meet in the lobby of the Tokyo Hilton early the next morning for the flight to Okinawa.

Shining with excitement, my new friend and I joined the group waiting in the lobby for the bus to the airport. Then the Colonel said, "Stand down everybody, there is an hour hold on the bus." The children played with young Marines and got a few more battle ribbons. The hotel bar had opened, and when we were informed of another hold, the Colonel decided we would wait there. A third trip out to the lobby for the bus-- another wait. The baby had burped milk on the Captain's uniform; the Marines, most of them eighteen years old, were playing with Becky, Wendy, and Kevin. My new friend and I were beginning to move from upset to feeling pretty good. Back to the bar we all went. At the next call we got on the bus and made it to the plane. Then the waits, hour by hour started again. By this time, a Sergeant and I had a bet going on whether we would get to Naha that day. I won.

Coming down the metal steps from the plane at Naha AB, Okinawa, tranquilized with alcohol, I didn't even get upset when I realized Ronald wasn't there. Bonnie and C.B., friends from Stillwater, were standing on the deck waving like mad. "Ronald is due to land in about two hours," C.B. said. "He is still trying to get back from the U.S. In fact, he was just outside Tokyo last night. That plane he is flying has broken down everywhere."

Ronald landed; everyone was happy! A family again, R.D. took us--in his twelve-year-old Volkswagen with pieces of wood over the rusted out floor--up-island onto the Kakazu ridge to our new home. The house was a shock. It was roofless and not close to being finished. We were all too stunned to be upset. One night in a borrowed room, and then the family had three wonderful days at Okuma, the Officers' Rest Camp on the north end of Okinawa. After that, R.D. began the squadron schedule of seventeen days in Vietnam and five days at Naha.

For the next six weeks we would move all over the island, living in whatever we could find until the house was finished. *And, I'm called the adult,* I thought after driving the kids to their new school in an old WW II prison camp. There, I had watched with awe as Becky, Wendy, and Kevin started their adjustment to a different world. "We are, for sure, on another adventure," I said to myself as I dodged my third Kamikaze cab driver. And, gathering my wits together, I began it.

Home On Kakazu Ridge

Futenma, Okinawa, 1966

Every time we dug a flowerbed, we had to call out the bomb squad. The American invasion of WW II--the Japanese called it the "Typhoon of Steel"--hit the island of Okinawa right here just south of Futenma on the Kakazu ridge where we lived.

Today, 1966, twenty-three small concrete houses looped back and forth down this upper section of the hill, housing, mostly, military families like ours. The total cost of the house Ronald had contracted for to get us to Okinawa was $5400--that was by the time the builder paid us back for the days past the contract due date it took to be finished.

Looking up the hill, you would see the road making the four loops from right to left and back, swooping down in a picturesque fashion that ended at our house. We lived right on the edge of the ridge overlooking the East China Sea. The 'right on the edge' was literal, as well as descriptive. You entered the house in the back, by the road. If you opened the front door and stepped out you would have tumbled straight down into the sugar cane fields below. I had a tiny porch with railings put on as I thought children, friends, and earthquakes could all be safety issues.

Earthquakes were an every day and night occurrence. We had three kinds. There were earthquakes that gave you a hard 'jerk.' There were earthquakes that existed as loud, amazingly stereophonic sounds like a phantom train swiftly moving through your space. They would start on the far right and roar on past, the sound going eerily through you to be lost out in the distance. Then there were the jellyrolls where the earth beneath your feet started to undulate like a bowl of Jell-O poked by a giant finger. Every morning, I would go into my living room and count the new cracks in the walls. It bothered me for a while, but the only person that had been hurt in years in an earthquake was a G.I. who jumped out of his second floor barracks window, and broke his leg.

Since we were situated at the bottom of this housing unit, the heavy tropical rains would pour off the road and yards above us reaching flood condition at my house. Two times, I opened that back door so floodwater could flow through the house, over the little porch, cascading down to the sugar cane fields below. I managed to laugh at the first experience until I had to shovel out the half-foot of mud in the house. The second time, the man that brought to me the wall air conditioning and heating unit that I had just bought from his house sale said, "My God! This is awful! Can I help?"

"Actually," I said, sliding in the mud, "I've been through this before. Your air conditioning unit will be useful fighting the mold."

"Do you mind," he said, as a shoe was sucked off in the kitchen, "if I tell my wife about this?"

"No I don't mind. Why would you even ask?"

"She has gone back to the states. Okinawa was too tough," he said, looking around in amazement at what was left of my living room, "and she never saw anything like this."

"And I'm not going to see this again," I said to R. D. when he arrived home from Vietnam. So we had a concrete topped canal system built around three sides of the house to channel the water and pour it off by the porch. It was fun to explain to friends, people new to the island, and our stateside family that this $5400 house had a $700 canal system around it.

I didn't think living in Okinawa was tough, I thought it was charming. "What are they doing? I said, as I stood on that concrete canal system and looked up the hill. Last week, the blue workmen (everyone official wore blue) had come and put in the telephone poles along the edge of the road, marching them down to our house. I was watching the desperately wanted phone line being slung over the poles starting at the very top of the hill. They were bringing it toward us, the line draping over each pole, swooping down to the ground in between, then up and over the next pole.

"What are they doing?" Susan, my neighbor, said, as she joined me staring in disbelief as the phone line continued to head our way.

"Okasan," what are they doing?" said Yukie, my maid, joining us.

"I'm afraid to say," I said, as I watched the road above me filling up with curious women, children, and maids.

Finally, the little men in blue started down our street throwing the phone line over the poles until they reached the one in front of our house. Then all stopped as they chatted with

Yukie; she started to laugh and waved me over. One man took hold of the end of the phone line, another grabbed him by the waist. The four lined up holding to each other and looked over their shoulders, expectantly, at me. The last in the odd conga line patted his waist and grinned. So I grabbed him. Susan came over, Yukie, and the children, and laughing we all started to pull. It was a ridiculous idea. But, down the hill, willing to seem foolish and sharing our laughter, came all the rest of the neighborhood. The men pulled; and we pulled with them. The phone line tightened pole by pole, and up it went. We did it! It was another happy day, and another excuse for a party.

There were a lot of impromptu parties as we learned to relax and enjoy living with these quite practical but child-like Okinawans. Our men were gone most of the time 'in country,' that meant they worked at whatever they did in Vietnam--some were Army Rangers based at Ft Buckner, or Marines based at Futenma, but, most, like R.D., were pilots based at Naha AB.

This neighborhood of women and children had become an extended family. We were beginning, in American slang, to 'roll with the punches'--and, with the Okinawans as an example, 'to have fun where you find it.' Like the day a big water pipe that was running underground in the sugarcane field below us broke. A fountain rose fifteen feet high into the air, and we lost the water to our houses. It didn't take long before women, children, and maids were lining the four loops of road coming down the hill. All of us were paying attention as little blue trucks with little blue men converged in the cane field.

Our watchfulness was based in self-interest, as well as curiosity, as the island was in water rationing. Okinawa planned on four typhoons a year to keep the water reservoirs full. We hadn't had a typhoon in two years. Our water had been turned off every night and back on in the morning for weeks. We were using drops of Clorox in it for regular use, and boiling it for drinking. Now, we got pots, pans, bowls, anything we could find, and all converged on the fountain to try and fill up. Everyone laughed and got soaked; and we all ended up playing as we got what water we could. The fountain flowed for five days as the island utility couldn't figure out how to turn it off. I told Ronald, when he came home, that happiness went from having ice cubes to having a flushed potty.

We were all lucky that no one in that cane field got bit by a habu. The habu was a snake, a pit viper that was found in the sugar cane fields. Its poison was neurotoxic and would kill you pretty quick. We were very careful, especially at night, for the habu liked our warm concrete. One afternoon, the workmen came and got us so we could watch habu eggs hatch. My children, Susan, Yuki, and I sat on top of the concrete wastewater system built into the side of the hill at the end of our street. The nest was right below us. As the little snakes broke through their leathery eggs and started away, the men politely killed them.

The workers often made off with our children, and they found my two red-headed boys interesting. They would fill up their blue trucks and take them to the village for an afternoon. Becky, Wendy, and Kevin always came home sucking on salty plums and glowing with their good time.

Okinawans loved children. Only women new to the island would make the mistake of taking a child with them to the beauty shop (Getting your hair done cost $1.50.). If someone did, we all were abandoned, our hair in curlers or full of soap--no longer important to anyone. The shop stopped to play with the child.

Okinawan girls, in their teens, found this small housing unit of American families whose husbands were gone most of the time. Wanting to practice their English, and curious, they would just show up. We were fascinated with each other. If a husband was at home, they would go to another house. It got to be expected and fun. Asuka was at my house often for a weekend. I finally realized she was hitchhiking all the way down from the north end of the island. One Saturday afternoon, she arrived visibly disturbed. "Asuka," I said, "what's the matter?"

"Okasan, I just came through Futenma and young American men were singing and marching through the streets. I asked who they were and a man said they were Marines and they would go to war. Okasan, is that true?"

"Yes, Asuka. That's true."

"Okasan, they looked so young. I asked the man and he said they are eighteen years old. Okasan, is that true?"

"Yes, Asuka."

"Okasan," Asuka said, as she started to cry, "They are too young."

"Yes," I said, as I started to cry with her, "They are too young."

I loved the Okinawans. This island was populated with wonderful people and every day was interesting and fun. Repeatedly, I groaned because I didn't have a camera. One day, we were coming home from Okuma, at the north end of the island, and saw this huge pig right at the edge of the road with his nose pointed to the other side. An older Okinawan man, in brown kimono and sandals, had hold of the pig's tail with both hands. The man's whole body was leaning back almost to the ground--his heels digging into the dirt as the pig strained to cross the road. Just as we passed, the man let go and fell with a big puff of dust and the pig ran safely across the road. "They get the job done," R.D. said, as the children and I laughed.

The nursery where we got our plants for the yard was truly beautiful. Rock walls layered up the hill as only the Asians can make them do, spilling over with greenery, nearly smothered in flowers of all colors. A small, brown, traditional Okinawan house with its curved tile roof sat in the northwest quadrant like an artist had placed it in his painting. This day, I was to realize that sometimes the eye, mind, and heart can be your camera. As I got out of the car I looked up and alone on the hill were two men. They were strolling together, in concentrated conversation, down the walk that meandered through those flowers. It was the little gardener, in kimono and straw hat, and a tall monk, in brown robes with a large wood cross hanging from his belt of rope. I really felt the 'click' as that picture was taken; I believe I will see it forever.

I loved Okinawa. The island, 67 miles long by 7 miles wide, rose out of a coral sea that was exotically beautiful. As scuba lessons were given by the military, R.D. and I decided to take them. I felt a little unreal, like I was in a movie, as we were required to wear a knife strapped to one leg and boots. "Never, never," said our instructor, "pick up anything in these seas with your bare hands as many of the critters here are neurotoxic. And watch out for sea snakes."

The alphabet cone, pretty, small, and deadly, was a coveted shell. We kept a bag of some sort and kitchen tongs stuck in our belts to pick up shells if you just had to have one. I left most of them alone believing that just being in their alien world was a gift. It was awesome to swim slowly above a spider conch, watching through your mask its green, muscular body--pink tinged shell on top--undulate over the sand; its eyes on the end of long green stalks waving to some sort of musical counterpoint that I couldn't hear.

A trip to a deep bay was special. We would climb down a cliff clanking with gear, and take a small wood boat out. Over the side in a backward splash and kicking once to lift my body out of the water, I would slowly sink, watching--as the warm, clear water rose gently up the outside of my mask--the rock of the cliff changing into a solid bank of thousands of corals. The colors were unbelievable from lavenders to rose to rust. The fish in bright yellows, reds, and iridescent blues moved lazily around me, occasionally touching, unconcerned with the strange thing in their sea. That fantastic underwater wall of corals went on and on forever, becoming blue and mysterious as it finally disappeared into the depths of the sea. I would move a flipper slightly, rotating within my crystal bubble, melding with the light that sprayed in all directions around me--wondering vaguely which direction was up, deciding, but not really caring. Then I would see my air bubbles going off at a tangent, and, realizing how wrong I had been, with an amused snort send a bunch more bubbles rushing after them. That small touch of reality over, I would let the warm buoyant water beguile me again into the beauty and comfort of its womb.

The drive home from the bay was on the main road of the island and sure to un-relax you as it was full of what we called "kamikaze cab drivers." As the island speed limit was 35 mph, no one was ever really hurt in the constant wave of accidents. The base commander at Naha decided to stop the problems caused by his military dependents--that meant us, the wives. He declared that for every accident a wife was in, the husband would have to go to driving school. The accident rate went way down. Immediately.

The one four-stop juncture on the road from Naha AB to up-island, where we lived, had a little policeman directing traffic who belonged in vaudeville. All in blue, he stood on a box in the middle of the road with his whistle at the ready in his mouth. Often his directions would be given with his whole body as he pointed by standing on one leg, that arm pointing in the direction that he wanted you to go, and the other arm and leg in the air pointing back: a graceful ballet position. Once I saw him stop all four roads of traffic. Getting off the box, he went to the side of one car in front, taking the hand of the young woman driving it, gallantly kissing it, and going back to his box--a whistle, and the amused and entertained drivers were on their way.

Later one evening in Naha City, we got stuck behind a drunk Okinawan waving his bottle of sake in the air before him, and singing as he weaved right down the middle of the road -- buses and cars stacking up behind him and honking in frustration. Finally, relaxing in our laughter, we let him lead our crazy parade.

On another evening, I got caught in a real parade in the city of Kadena. We lived in Okinawa from 1966 through 1969, and the politics to get the U.S. to give the island back to Japan had been heating up (The US returned it in '72.). I was driving home from a friend's house on Kadena AB. As the children and I got in the city, the police stopped us to let a parade come through. The street was full of lanterns, men with red bands tied around their foreheads beating drums, and lovely girls in full dress kimonos. It was quite a show, but I couldn't believe the huge banners they carried. These banners reached from one side of the street to the other; they were enormous, and green, and American dollar bills. I was amused for the whole thirty-minute drive home. It was obvious which side these new capitalists were on and, in the way of Okinawans, they made their point. Ronald would enjoy this story when he got home.

With the squadron flying in Vietnam for seventeen days, then when back working on the base for five days, there was a lot of extra stress on the families. It didn't take long for the women to start banding together to cope with their unusual lives. The squadron commander's wife called a meeting. "There are some problems," she said. "The old heads are doing O.K., but they live on base. It's the families living off base, especially the new ones, that need our attention. What about meeting each family as they arrive and helping them get settled? We could register the kids for school, and give everyone a chance to start by understanding a little of the culture of this island. How about it?" We all agreed, a list was made up of greeters, and the welcoming process began.

One of the realities of living off base was the 'steally boy'; these were the young Okinawan boys that would come into your house at night and steal whatever they wanted. We had shipped our little black Schnauzer, Gretchen, from the states and kept her in the house. I had never been hit as Gretchen barked, and for some reason she hated male Okinawans. One family in our neighborhood tried a local dog, Sam, a large yellow mutt who became the focus of round-eyed interest from the children when the adults began to refer to him as Syphilis Sam. Old S.S.

was kept outside and that didn't help at all where the 'steally boys' were concerned.

These 'steally boys' were good. They would come into your house at night and go directly to unlock the door out, then as our schedules were crazy because our men were pilots, come into your bedroom and turn off the alarm clock by your bed. You never knew a thing until the next morning. Thank goodness no one ever got hurt. Still, to have a visit from a 'steally boy' was a common and unsettling occurrence.

I had been asked to meet a new family for a friend that couldn't, as she was going to be off island. The wife seemed shy, but I got them settled and the children, a boy, nine, and girl, seven, in school. Later, the wife called me, disturbed; she had heard about the 'steally boys.' I had her over for coffee, made light of it, and told her about Gretchen, suggesting she try a dog if that would make her feel better. Several weeks went by and the Base called--would I come help as the children knew me? She had been found dead that morning; they had her husband on his way back from Vietnam.

This was the strangest time. I cleaned up their house and tried to keep the children from bouncing off all the walls. In every closet, I found plastic sacks of towels and stuff with the price tags on. Sacks were under beds and in the cabinets. There were tranquilizers everywhere. *Something was very wrong*, I thought.

When her husband arrived, he sat in shock on the couch reading out loud a letter from her, rerouted back from Vietnam, that had just been given to him. The small group in the living room had trouble even breathing as he read and cried. She was so afraid. Everything in Okinawa was strange and her fears were all over the place.

The military police said she had called them that night and reported something. They had gone out and not found a thing. She called again; they responded. Later, when they called to talk to her, a child said mother was asleep and they couldn't wake her. Someone was sent out to check. She was dead; her heart had just stopped. Her husband, holding the letter in his shaking hands and tears running down his face, said over and over again, "Can a person die of fear?" We just sat there mute, our hearts asking the same question.

All our children went to schools that were excellent because the teachers were. The series of low, gray, unpainted, wood buildings where my children went had been a prison, and then a hospital. My first day helping in Becky's class, we were in monsoonal rains, and I found the classroom under about a foot of water. The teacher, who was young, adventurous, and very good, was sitting cross legged on her desk reading to the students who were sitting on the back of their old fashioned desk chairs with their feet in the seat. It looked like everyone was having a good time, so I just waded in and joined them.

Wendy volunteered me to help with his 5th grade class Roman Orgy. When I got there, all the desks were gone, and the teacher, with the help of the always willing G.I.s, had gotten mattresses from the barracks. The boys, in togas made of sheets, were laying on them. The girls, in short pieces of sheet with rope belts, were bringing the food in on trays and serving grape juice wine. The class musicians played a discordant sound from a corner of the room. I was alarmed when I went out the back of the building and found a young man sticking his finger in his throat and throwing up. "Are you all right? Can I do something?" I said, gearing up to take charge as he spewed up some half eaten grapes and something else I wasn't sure about.

The expression of concern I gave got back a look of pure disgust. "This is what you do in Roman orgies," he said, and to my amusement went back in to eat some more.

An eclectic education had been pouring into our family and we were getting ready to add a little spice. Susan came over bursting with news. "The guys say they have sold their house to a big businessman in Naha City. They think it's for his mistress." 'The guys' were four bachelors that lived directly across the street from me and were moving on base. I looked out my kitchen window at their house; and Susan lived next door to them.

"Oh! Boy! I've been wondering about that big car with the black windows," I said. "I've seen it stopping on our road several times. Won't this be interesting?" About then there was a knock on my door, and an Okinawan gentleman, who said he represented the buyer, asked to speak to us. We were informed that the person moving in did not speak English and did not want to be disturbed.

Susan came over every day to find out what was going on for my kitchen window was a fount of information. A smaller black car would drive in and a beautiful oriental lady, always dressed in a kimono, would walk into the house. The driver would wash the car and then follow her. Very late one night, I noticed lights at the top of the hill and saw a cab let the lady out and pull away. She stood there for quite some time and then walked down to her house. "Wow! Susan, you should have seen that kimono. It must have cost over a 1000 dollars!"

"I saw her yesterday," Susan said. "She was walking down the hill on those wooden clogs, and in a cotton daytime kimono with a jacket that was smashing."

Our curiosity continued unabated until Halloween and my children decided to go trick-or-treating. Ignoring their mother, they stopped at the house across the street. The beautiful young woman gave each of them their first Japanese persimmon. This allowed me a chance to say, "Thank you," and Susan to say "Hello, I live next door." Before long, Matsuko, our new friend, wanted to learn a little English and how to cook a hamburger. In exchange, she would show us all her kimonos. Matsuko was put on this street and in our neighborhood on purpose; and she was careful not to let even the cab drivers know where she lived. Her driver, she told us, was a cousin and not available all the time.

"My friends in Boston will never believe this," said Susan, as we watched in awe as another thousand-dollar-kimono minced on those wooden clogs up the street. "A real geisha, and she says I'm her friend. Wow!"

"Isn't living on Okinawa fun?" I said, knowing Susan was thinking about going back to the states.

"Today it is," she said, as leaving, she patted me on the head, "but just wait until tomorrow."

Tomorrow came. First, I heard the shouting in the neighborhood, and then Yukie ran in with the children. "Okasan, Okasan," she said, running around and closing windows, "quick, quick!"

Kevin hollered for me to look outside. "What is that?" I said, looking at a large black cloud coming toward us.

"Okasan, termites! They come!"

Oh! My God! I've read about this in books, I thought as we all ran around, running into each other and stuffing towels under the doors. The world outside turned dark, and the sound of millions of tiny bodies hitting windows and house filled our ears. Then termites began to come in.

"Where? Where?" I yelled, feeling a little hysteria was allowed and slapping at termites as they flew around me.

"There!" said Becky, pointing at the new ill fitted wall air conditioner. Around it and through it, hundreds and hundreds of termites swarmed in like gray smoke, sizzling like electrified genies.

We slapped, hit, sprayed, and cussed termites. Finally, the black cloud flew through us and continued on its way. As light returned in the windows, I slid down the wall to sit on the floor next to an exhausted Yukie and, giving her a small relieved smile, said, "Thank God, that's over."

"Not over," she said, looking right into my eyes and not returning my smile. "Okasan," she said, knocking a couple of termites off her arm as she got up, "not over."

And it wasn't. In too short a time, small piles of sawdust appeared on the floor. We soon had to replace most of the door jams in our concrete block house, and the wood around the windows. When I found piles of saw dust under the wood fruit on the table and under some of the chairs, something had to be done. We ended up getting our most important acquisition in the three years on Okinawa: our Gecko.

"I keep a Gecko under the mosquito netting where I sleep in Nam; they stay out of your way and eat all the bugs," R.D. said, as he presented the small box. In it was a tiny Gecko that was to live in our house. It stayed high up, right where the wall joined the ceiling, making its clicking sound, and obviously doing a great job. We didn't have any more problems with bugs of any type and our Gecko got huge. Gretchen barked her head off, running around the living room trying to make it come down and play. For the rest of Gretchen's life, we could set her off by clicking our tongue in our mouth, and saying, "Gretchen! Gecko! Gecko!" Around and around the living rooms of New Mexico, Ohio, and California she would go, wistfully looking up and barking--even in her old age remembering and wanting to be excited again.

Monuments

Naha, Okinawa, 1967

"These idiots are going to kill my Gecko!" I said, feeling a surge of protective anger. On Naha AB, the military required us, monthly, to remove everything out of cabinets and closets so they could come and spray pesticides. "Gecko lives with us and eats all our bugs. He's our friend. They are not going to do this." One month in our first housing on a base, and I was already at war with the military.

For a couple of times when the airman came to spray, I battled, trying out no, arguing, and some hollering. Afraid that I would lose the war, I enlisted the children, and we all resorted to tears and sobbing. That did it. The airman that was supposed to spray simply chose not to come back to our house for the eighteen months we lived there. I felt truly grateful for my Gecko as we were bug free. And I felt bad for a friend as I watched a line of strange and menacing bugs march up the bathroom wall of her house that got that monthly spraying.

Living on base may not have been as interesting as up-island, but it was more convenient for all the family. The children, especially, were excited to be able to join the base swim team. Still, in measuring twelve-year-old Becky for her swimsuit, I became slightly depressed to learn that her breast, waist, and hip measurements were all nineteen inches.

Becky was taking to swimming with a passion, riding her bicycle to every class through the rain and sun of our tropical weather. I suspected this had something to do with the cute airman that was one of the instructors. This day she tried to get into the house without me noticing her tears. "Becky, honey, what's the matter?" Her tears turned into sobs. "Come on, you can tell Momma." Between the sobs and gulps, the story was told of her swim class that day.

"Becky," said Skip, the adored young instructor, "stand sideways and stick out your tongue." And when she did, that insensitive young man said, "Now, you look like a zipper." Becky was devastated. I had a couple of tears myself as I patted her and murmured words of encouragement. This process of growing up may be tough, but it's winnable. My daughter received the swim trophy that season for "most improved."

Bonding with Becky was part of the reason that I agreed to take on the role of Girl Scout leader. There was an art show of local artists going on at the museum in Naha City. *This*, I thought, *would be a great cultural experience and good for the development of the girls.* It also was an opportunity to see something wonderful as Okinawans were artists to a level that I found exciting. The base commander was talked out of a bus to take our Troop to the museum, and Sunday afternoon we arrived.

The paintings hung on the huge walls of the central room of the museum. A two-inch thick crimson velvet rope marked out the walkway along the wall and forced the viewers to move in a single file around the room to see the art. I tumbled from excitement to disappointment as most of the paintings were depressing--many were of atomic bombs and the aftermath. We were on an island that was one of the most beautiful on earth and the artists who lived here ignored it. My opinion of the show and the fact that I was responsible for these new young Scouts had increased my stress level. Making what positive comments I could, I led my troop around the room with the girls following behind me and my assistant leader at the end of our little line. We were doing well moving in our single file until about five feet from the end of the crimson velvet rope where I stopped, stunned. In front of me was a group of eight very clear, very graphic, framed oil paintings placed on the wall as they might have been on a body. The body would have been a male. One showed an ear and part of a jaw and neck. One was a section of a shoulder. One was a hand. Down close to the floor, another framed painting was of some toes and part of an ankle. You get the idea. Right in front of me, just below my eye level, was a framed excellent rendering of a penis in full bloom. *Oh my God,* I thought, *why me?* Then, I tried to come up with something clever to do or say, and came up with an inane, "Let's move along girls." There were one or two snickers, but other than that we finished the show in silence--mine, grim.

Parents can be real trouble, I thought, *and the base commander wasn't going to be happy either.* For several days, I expected the phone to ring and for things to blow up. But nothing happened, although, we did get several new members to our troop and I noticed the girls had a tendency to look at me and laugh.

Learning to cope and to 'have fun where you find it,' the lessons of Okinawa were important skills. The pilots in this squadron (41st ATS) spent a three-month tour each year flying Blind Bat, a squadron of unmarked black planes out of Ubon,

Thailand. On our T.V., the U.S. Ambassador told the media that America was not flying over Cambodia or China. "He's lying," R.D. said, snorting in disgust, "I've been to both places."

Ronald would come home from Vietnam tired, but hyper and full of stories, most of them funny. He told about smelling smoke and sending his slightly hysterical flight engineer to the back of the plane to make the Korean troops put out the fires they lit in the cargo area for tea. Then the Koreans got even by breaking out their kimchee pots and stinking up everything. One trip, R.D. was to transport a bunch of hardened Marines. His co-pilot came into the cockpit for advice having had words with a young Marine who said his scroungy yellow puppy was getting on the plane with him. Looking out the window and seeing a tough, dirty, 6'3" Marine with puppy on rope in one hand and M-16 in the other hand, Ronald decided to revise the rules. "If you want to tell him that he can't have his dog on board, you can, but I wouldn't bring it up," he told his co-pilot.

Often, R.D. would land on a strange airfield, and have a small unit of Army Rangers with blackened faces move out of the jungle, then quietly get off in another place in civilian clothes--or have them get on in civvies and get off in jungle gear. "Always, in an eerie silence." One time he was spooked as he felt he transported a unit of North Vietnamese.

For the most part, the guys kept quiet about the bad stuff. It would be in Los Angeles eight years later, and after retirement, that I heard different stories. Ronald, in marketing for Lear Sigler, had some of our Air Force friends in so I was included in this evening out. In the bar after dinner, they got started telling war stories. Making myself as small as possible and not moving, in silence I listened. Ronald told about flying at night over Vietnam where an oriental version of Moscow Molly would talk to him by name: "Hello, Major Dudley. We know where you are, and what you are doing. Aren't you lonely up there? Afraid we're going to shoot you down? Why don't you talk to me?"

R.D. said, "We would come back to the base for the debriefing after a flight and act cool like John Wayne. I would say, 'We took ten hits in the fuselage and eight hits in the wings.' Then we would go to the Officers Club and order a triple martini." Every pilot kept, in a flight suit pocket, a piece of plastic tubing supplied by the nurses. They used this tubing to down their martinis because their hands would be shaking so hard they could not hold their drinks.

"I was flying ammunition into the Marines in one of the battles of Khe Sanh," Ronald said, as he sipped his scotch. "We would come in scared, landing hot, and under heavy fire. Those Marines would be just out of ammunition. They would board my plane, grabbing ammo as they loaded the dead and dying. I've never seen anything like it. We kept our engines running, getting in and out as fast as possible. The squadron finally took me off flight status. I got so I couldn't sleep; it was the smell of the dead."

We didn't know it was Khe Sanh that night Shirley Hagerty and I sat on the concrete steps that led up the hill to our yards. We were just talking and enjoying a beautiful Okinawan moon that veiled the base and runways below us in blue light. Sirens began to sound and the military police drove through the housing areas with loud speakers. There was an emergency. A battle was going on in Nam, and they would be out of blood in a few hours. A whole base turned out that night. Everyone that could got into the buses to go up island to Kadena AB, where they gave blood to be put into our planes and sent straight to Vietnam.

Toward the end of our tour, the Hagertys and Dudleys went together to see Suicide Cliffs, the park at the south end of the island where so many people died as the WW II Battle of Okinawa ended. The park was breathtakingly beautiful. It stopped at cliffs that fell 300 ft. down into an edge of black rocks that appeared and disappeared as they were battered by the great white froth of the blue-green Pacific Ocean on your left, and the East China Sea on your right.

The Battle for Okinawa was horrendous--12,000 Americans, 107,000 Japanese, and 150,000 Okinawans died on this 67 by 7 mile wide island in 85 days. This battle was to be the worst and the last in the Pacific. Some historians suggest it was this horrifying death toll and the number of suicides involved that convinced President Truman to use the atom bomb on Japan. Truman was said to have been worried that an invasion of the Mother Island would be "an Okinawa from one end of Japan to another."

Suicide Cliffs was where that war on Okinawa ended; the Japanese commanders committed hari-kari here. Knowing that the battle had come in where we used to live near Futenma and pushed south, and that many people committed suicide here was one thing, but the emotional reality of this place was simply overwhelming. It sent out a message I had felt before as a child standing on the front porch of General Lee's home: Arlington, looking over the sea of plain white crosses below, and crying in grief for everyone. The monuments of stark black and white in this park break your heart, for they honor the 10,000 people who committed suicide here that June of 1945 by grenade, hari-kari, or jumping off the cliffs.

Peace was what one huge monument radiated as it sat on the edge of the cliffs and looked out at its eternal view of the sea. That's why I had moved to stand beside it and lay my hands on the warm stone. Coming out of the Cave of the Virgins, where 219 high school girls and 18 instructors had all committed suicide, tears were acceptable. But, I needed a moment with this monument and those turquoise seas before I joined my boisterous family. Turning to locate Ronald and our children, I found myself looking directly at the wood walk that went the length of the park. It was empty except for a young American G.I., in his army khakis, and a young Okinawan girl, in her short navy skirt and white blouse. They were laughing and holding hands. In their other hand, they each had a bottle of Coca-Cola. A brief moment of agony flowed through my whole body for the lives lost--it had only been twenty-two years. *God forgive us all*, I thought, and click went my internal camera--another picture, this one framed in beauty, grief, and regret.

Today, near the end of our three-year tour on Okinawa I was wasting too much time trying to understand my life. The Base had announced that we were experiencing 110% humidity. We had water running down the inside of our walls, and the electric outlets on the floor were sputtering. "Damn monsoonal rains." I was sliding around in the thin glaze of water on the floor--we had had ninety inches of rain in the last three months. "Damn military." Orders were here for our next base: Holloman, AFB, Alamogordo, N.M.--ten miles off the White Sands National Monument. Gearing up to mop at the water, and clean out the closets, I found a smile and felt a tiny surge of excitement. My

Gecko, from his perch high on the dripping wall, eyed all this activity with curiosity. "We are going to miss you," I said sincerely, as he scampered after an errant bug. *At least*, I thought on a positive note, *these next few years should be dry.*

Changes

Alamogordo, New Mexico, 1969
Dayton, Ohio, 1971

I thought I was going to have a heart attack. This was one of the scariest things I had ever done: driving a car on an insane California freeway after living three years on an island, 67 miles long and 7 miles wide, where the maximum speed was 35 miles per hour.

We came back to the states through San Francisco. Ronald went straight to Holloman, AFB, Alamogordo, N.M. to sign in, hoping for base housing. The children and I flew to Mom and Dad in Florida. There, I was to get Gretchen, our little black Schnauzer, out of customs, and start looking for a car so the family could drive back to New Mexico.

"We just got back to the States," I said to every car dealership on the southwest coast of Florida. "I have three kids, a dog, and ten suitcases to drive to Alamogordo N.M. What have you got?" The answers were depressing. "Ronald," I said, when he arrived, "these people aren't listening to me. This is a bummer. You should see what they are trying to sell us." So R.D. and I started over and it stayed depressing until we walked into a dealership in Venice.

"Oh! My god! There you are," said an excited salesman, "the lady that has three kids, a dog, and ten suitcases. I didn't know how to find you. It came in! Just what you want!" And, it was. We bought a three-year-old yellow Chrysler New Yorker. You could put twenty suitcases in that trunk. The car was huge. You just felt it lay out and purr when you hit eighty miles an hour. Our family loved it. Four years later when we traded it in for a Volkswagen Club Car, the Chrysler blew its motor a mile from our house. The car dealer trying to drive it away was disgusted and yelled bad words at Ronald. But the family understood. We sincerely believed that this was not really a mechanical breakdown; it was a suicide.

My head was pure agony, and there was blood all over my pillow. "Good morning, and welcome to the high desert. We're over 4,000 ft. here, where you only have ten inches of rain a year," R.D. said, as he handed me several aspirins and a glass of water. "The kids are in the same shape you are. I've already called, and the flight surgeon's office is expecting you. As soon as you can, my dear, you are to get over there."

The doctors decided our bodies were upset. Not Ronald's, for he had flown to other climates in the three years we lived on Okinawa. For us, it was a combination of the high and dry of our new base and the ninety inches of rain in the three months before we left our tropical island. After several tries, the medical community solved the severe nighttime nosebleeds by putting a humidifier in the house for our first six months on base.

I wish the rest of our problems had been as easy to solve. Ronald changed, or time changed, or we changed--because something in our life began to shift after Vietnam. I had heard this type of a complaint before from military wives when their loved ones have been in a war. Now it was mine.

The effects of Vietnam seemed to have been a little squirrelier emotionally than most. For the first time in my world, I felt a disturbance in the air around our military family. I felt a loss of solidarity, in some way, in my life. I've heard people talk about what happens to behavior when a society loses faith in the "civil contract" they feel they have with their community or their government. That may have been part of it. We began to walk through a fog of realization that this government didn't tell the truth. We began to see the use of drugs. Military friends of ours who were against the war were sure the FBI checked their mail.

Then there were the really sickening intimidating calls to the wives and families of the military by the nastier part of the anti-Vietnam movement. With increasing fervor, we banded together trying to make up for that disturbance. Even the young widows that I knew chose to stay close to a base rather than move to a biological family that couldn't understand their feelings. Most of my women friends, when Ronald was flying in Vietnam, would have wanted to shoot Nixon themselves if their husband had been killed. We didn't talk about it much. Our guys, as far as we were concerned, were just doing their job.

On Holloman, Ronald was with the Maverick Missile Test Division, part of the Missile Development Center. Everyone was amused, and told bad jokes about the guys, for they had the only tanks in the Air Force. R.D. took Wendy and Kevin out into the desert and let them drive one. The boys decided, either from a movie or a T.V show, that the battle ribbons they found in the tank were German. R.D. winked at me and made hand signals to keep quiet. We both knew that at one of the formal military functions a year before this, a friend of ours--a squadron 'hot-dog' with lots of ribbons--had gotten drunk and drove a tank up the steps of the Officers Club. This must have been the tank.

The Air Tactical Command that shared the base with the missile section was losing a lot more pilots than we did in Nam. The number of crashes got so bad that the Commander ordered his men to write wills and check their insurance. The women took classes in the five stages of grief: denial, anger, bargaining, depression, and acceptance. This invaluable information quickly spilled through all the women on that base. We learned that you had to go through each stage, although in your own way and at your own pace, or you got stuck in one and didn't get over it. This understanding, in many ways, turned out to be a great survival gift for the rest of my life.

I fell back on my basic methods of coping: friends, my piano, books, and PBS. The rest of the family managed, each in their own way.

Becky, with her pencils perfectly lined up on her desk and her panties perfectly folded into perfect squares--planned her life. She began to say, "When I'm 18…" She was talking, I think, about finally being able to do what she wanted; but, another reality hit two years later, when she was 18.

Kevin was always a delight: easy, funny, sincere. His first grade teacher had pointed out that he took care of everyone in his class; "fathered" was the word she used. His second grade teacher, seeming to be flummoxed, said, "Do you know, he tests out the highest in our class."

As Kevin was three years younger than Wendy, and a lot taller, I worried about this causing a problem. So I had a rule that Kevin did not get anything or do anything until at least a year after Wendy. I didn't know what else to do. About this time, Kevin had started singing his troubles. I will always remember one of Wendy's birthdays when he got a camera. Kevin, trying not to show how badly he wanted a camera, went off by himself. I hid, wet eyed, and listened to him. "I don't need a camera. My eyes can see me. I know what I look like," he sang.

In a year from this day and on another base, R. D. and I would be in the orthodontist's office talking about Kevin's teeth. Our Dentist said, "What do you want first--the good news, or the bad news?

"Give me the good news," said Ronald.

"It's going to cost you $1,500."

"Oh! My god! What's the bad news?" Ronald and I both exclaimed.

"We've x-rayed the bones in Kevin's hand; and he has four more years of growth."

Kevin would graduate from high school at 6 foot, 5 inches: the tallest boy in his class.

Wendy grew as his father had, he got his height after graduating from high school. Wendy would graduate from high school the shortest boy in the class.

In Alamogordo, Wendell had found out that you could have a motorcycle at 13. He decided, with all the energy and focus at his command, that he was to have one. I was the person in his way as I strongly believed that giving motorcycles or cars to children wasn't good for them.

Wendy's verbal battering campaign started when he woke up in the morning and stopped when he went to sleep at night. It began to take over and color my life. I needed help, but R.D. did not believe in this kind of thing. Finally, I insisted.

Wendy and I went to several meetings with a counselor. She called me in; "Mrs. Dudley, you have a problem," she said. "Wendell has decided that he has to separate mother and father to get what he wants. This is a very intelligent child and he knows exactly what he is doing. I'm sorry that I must tell you that you can never protect yourself or enter into it in anyway; if you do, you have lost and things will only get worse."

"What do I do? That's why we are here. I'm trying the best I can right now."

"You must trust to your husband's good judgment. When Wendell starts, my advice to you is leave, just get out of the house. Go for a walk." That is what I did, but for a long time it left me feeling that in my family, I was just a cook and maid.

Wendell got his motorcycle.

Old friends, the Hansons, who lived on Okinawa with us-- Syphilis Sam had been their dog--were coming to Holloman. Although we already had orders, it was great to overlap for a few weeks. They flew from El Paso into Alamogordo in a small plane over some very desolate desert country. All five children were crying by the time they landed. We gave hugs, agreeing that we were isolated, that the country they flew over was different, and not pretty and green like Okinawa. We offered advice and support, wished them the best, and told them we had our new assignment.

"We are going to Wright-Patterson, AFB, Dayton, Ohio. You'll like it," R.D. said, "the Tolles are there." I was getting supper ready, so he announced the news and quickly left the room.

"Louise, I'm going to see Louise again! Louise, Charlie Fred, Misty, Hazel Mae. It will be wonderful!" I said, waltzing around the kitchen with an empty pot. I waltzed to the theme from Dr. Zhivago. I was remembering a golden afternoon on Okinawa at Louise's house: the tropical sun sinking into the East China Sea, Charlie Fred and Ronald at their very best, the conversation and cocktails flowing, and Misty dancing to this lovely music. It was a glorious, glorious, precious memory.

"Aw, Mom, what are you doing? When is supper ready?"

"Wendy, we are going to Dayton. We will see the Tolles again. Isn't that great?"

"Aw, Mom, I'm hungry," Wendy said exuding exasperation. I got busy with the cooking, but my mind was back in Okinawa with Louise.

I met Louise Tolle at the Unitarian Fellowship. We were both delighted to find out that we lived up-island, just across the sugar cane fields, and on around the Kakazu Ridge from each other. R.D. and Charlie Fred were in the same squadron at Naha. Misty, their ten-year-old daughter, a budding ballet dancer, easily made friends with my children. And, tough-looking Hazel Mae, their German shepherd, proved to be a lovable scaredy-cat.

Louise dripped charm, loved intelligence and culture, believed in friends and laughter, had the taste of an artist--and integrated Dayton, Ohio.

The Tolles had come to Okinawa from Dayton. The military shipped Charlie Fred out, and Louise was left to sell their house and move the family. Alone, Louise Tolle sold the first house in a white neighborhood in Dayton to a black family. "They were nice people. They had saved up all that money," Louise said, as she sat my coffee in front of me. "I'm ashamed to say it, but it would have been easier if he were a lawyer or something. Instead he drove a bus, and she was a secretary to the school system. Sue, I had lived there nine years. My neighbors and friends, who I loved and I thought loved me, were vicious. Instantly, they hated me."

"Oh, Louise, I can't imagine how awful that must have been."

"The most difficult thing I did was to let Misty walk by herself to the school bus every morning. I sent Hazel Mae with her but still I was sick with fear. I must say the Unitarian Church helped. Friends came all day. They brought books, food, anything they could think of. It was their effort to have people around and not leave me completely alone."

We were sitting at the kitchen table with our coffee and a plate of cookies. I was reacting with no small amount of awe, as I had not heard this story.

"I called you to come over this morning because I needed someone. I just got a letter from my best friend and neighbor, the one who became so ugly. She has not spoken to me in all these years. I'm a little stunned," Louise said. She had tears in her eyes when she handed me an envelope.

It was a letter from her friend that simply said hello and how are you. A newspaper clipping from the Dayton paper fell out of the letter. It was headed: An Angel Named Tolle. "Oh, Louise, this is wonderful," I said, as I read, beginning to sniff in my effort not to cry. Dayton had set up a program to try and make the integration of their communities easier. A forum of four people went around to homeowner groups, civic organizations, churches--anywhere they could. They were a lawyer, minister, Louise's former friend and neighbor, and the lady who bought her house. The forum was set up for questions and answers but the ladies told personal stories of what happened to them. They talked about how they felt, what the real consequences were of having a black family move into your neighborhood--and about Louise. The title of their talk: An Angel Named Tolle.

Now, in Dayton, I needed Louise for I got depressed. We finally found out it was a sunshine issue. Sun lamps were put in over the kitchen counter and in the den and the problem was solved. After all the years in the tropics and the desert, the doctors said, my body was rebelling at the Dayton weather. Made sense to me. The weather people announced on the radio that in that month of December, Dayton had had a total of twelve hours of sunshine.

The weather did get better and Wendy decided that he would hike a section of the Ohio Buckeye Trail that followed an old barge canal through the woods outside the city. We studied the maps and found a farmer who would let you camp by a lake on his land, if you made reservations. For some reason, I decided, after lecturing myself on letting kids go and letting them have adventures and letting them grow up, that with two it would be safer and insisted that he take Kevin.

Early that June morning, backpacks loaded, they got out of the car in the woods where the road crossed the trail. "Wendy, I am staying home so I will be there if you need me. Call and I will come and get you. Be safe. Have fun." Then I went home to pace and worry.

Wendy called the next morning. "Mom, can you come get us? Kevin's sick."

"Oh, my God! Are you all right?"

"Yeah. Kevin's just sick. He's throwing up."

"Yes. I'll be right there," I said, trying not to panic, and wondering what awful thing had happened. "Where are you?"

"We are at a farmer's house on a dirt road, County Road 27, north of Dayton."

"Wendy, how will I find the house?"

"Oh, you can't miss it. They're burning two dead horses in the front yard. That's why Kevin's sick."

They had had an adventure all right. Mosquitoes were a terrible problem and after falling in the canal several times, the boys found a way out to a road and hitch-hiked to the farmer's house. The farmer let them pitch their tent at his lake. The mosquitoes were so bad that they spent the night in the lake, standing up to their necks in the water. While the boys ate several hamburgers at McDonald's, I counted sixty-four mosquito bites on Wendy and over a hundred on Kevin.

Louise came by to hear my story about the boys' hike, but she really wanted to urge me to go with her to night classes at Wright-State University. "Here are the results of the test I took. It just cost twenty dollars. They tell you what you would be good at. Come on Sue. I want you to go with me." We were sitting at my kitchen table where Louise had laid out her test results; she would make a great engineer, doctor, or lawyer.

"I'll think about it," I said, sipping my coffee.

Later I told Jeanne, another friend, about the tests. In three weeks, Jeanne and I sat at my kitchen table with her test results. Coffee was poured and we settled in so I could take a look. She would make a good secretary, nurse, or teacher. "Jeanne, this is not the same test that Louise had," I said, slowly handing the papers back to her.

"What do you mean, not the same test?'

"Jeanne, Louise tested high as an engineer, a lawyer, or a doctor. You're smarter than both of us. This is not the same test."

It wasn't the same test. This was 1973, and at this major university they gave one test to men--and another test to women. These tests had much different possibilities. When backed to the wall, the university authorities admitted that because she had an undergraduate degree in Math, they gave Louise the test normally given only to men.

Louise's demands for me to go to school with her were successful; and, she lit a dormant fire. Even though I thought we would be leaving Dayton shortly when Ronald retired, I ended up finishing three classes in Geography. The first was in earth science and ignited a passion in me that exists today.

Retirement was getting close. The family had dreamed and planned on going to Florida. Becky, so she could move with us, had arranged her senior year to graduate in December as Ronald was retiring in January. Becky, at 5' 10" and 121 lbs, had taken modeling classes and gone to New York for a weekend. I had made a Bill Blass, Vogue pattern, evening gown for this trip--and her senior prom. The gown was simply beautiful. It had long sleeves, a tiny belted waist, and double bias ruffles at the neck that went down very low in front. I used French seams throughout the whole dress and two layers of white silk chiffon in the graceful skirt. It was a work of art and took hours. Right before R.D.'s retirement, our family's plans changed: we would not be going to Florida. R.D. accepted a job with Lear Siegler. He would be at Hill, AFB, in Utah, for six months on a special missile project. Then, R.D. would go directly to Los Angeles. We were to stay in Dayton for the six months; I was to sell the house, and move us to L.A. All Becky's changes to her senior year were made unnecessary.

After Ronald left for Utah, I would sit in the living room horrified as Becky found out from her long-time steady boyfriend that because she had graduated in December and he thought she wouldn't be in Dayton for their senior prom, he had made another date. My daughter would not be going to her senior prom. She sat in our living room and sobbed and sobbed until I thought my heart would break. When I started to blubber, Becky, enraged, said, "What are *you* crying for?"

"My dress," I said, between sobs, "isn't going to the senior prom." It took years before Becky forgave her family for that disaster.

Retirement was almost here. R.D. had spent the day trying to get all his paperwork through the military bureaucracy. "This has been a tough experience," he said, as he came into the kitchen that evening. "I ran into a real idiot captain, and he wasn't going to sign my orders."

"My goodness, Ronald! What happened?"

"This stupid man said he wouldn't sign because I had never been to the required class on race relations. We call it Watermelon U. I said he was a dumb shit. I didn't need to go because I was retiring. Then we got into a shouting match, and the major came out of his office to find out what was going on. So the major and I got into it. I finally said I don't need to go to Watermelon U to understand how to get along with blacks. My god! I got two of them for Christmas when I was six years old."

"Ronald, you didn't," I said, horrified at my Alabama born and bred husband.

"Of course I did. The major just exploded and told the captain to sign my orders and to get me out of there."

"What did you mean, 'You got two for Christmas?'"

"Well, I did. When I was six years old, Mom and Dad were working for the cotton mill in town. They left Donnie and me on the farm with Grandpa. He didn't have any money to get presents for us for Christmas, so he got a sharecropper family with two children about our ages. He said they were our Christmas presents."

All the paper work did get signed. This was the day. The family sat proudly in the audience, and on the stage stood six Air Force officers. At a podium on the left, an officer read out the bases and commands that made up the military career of each man as he was retired. I found myself trying to stifle a laugh for I had just realized that the General who was handing out the retirement orders was wearing some sort of fuzzy gray slippers. Even in my amusement, I noticed that the list of commands that made up each officer's career was rather short. When they got to Lt. Col. Ronald Edward Dudley, that list was noticeably longer. "What's the matter, son?" said the general, handing R.D his retirement orders, and grinning as he listened to the number of moves and commands that made up R.D.'s twenty years in the military, "Couldn't you hold a job?

Afterwards

Los Angeles, California, 1974
Englewood, Florida, 1978
Gainesville, Florida, 1999

California was a kick! Newly civilians, we arrived in Los Angeles just as the City Council of Venice decided to close their very popular nude beach. Anyplace else I had lived would have had preachers preaching and people marching--but, not here. "Cars are slowing down and running into each other because people are gawking. Our nude beach is causing traffic jams," said the city council men. "We are going to have to close it."

"Yes," solemnly agreed everyone else, "can't have traffic jams." And, that was the end of the discussion.

I was in one of those 'What am I doing with my life?' moods after spending time crying in the shower (my private place) over a fight between Becky and Wendy. They were both in their upper teens and having a difficult time. "Enough of this," I muttered, stomping out to find something for me.

What I found was Pierce Jr. College. Hooray! I was going back to school! This was California just before Proposition 13 limited taxes, and their education system was wonderful. My total cost for a semester was two dollars and that was for a parking permit. At Pierce, I found two new passions: Oceanography and Mr. Clark's music classes.

Mr. Clark, a genius, was to retire in two years. I dove into Pierce's music school taking every class he taught. That lovely man, bless his heart, gave me an F in tonality while gently explaining that I was musical as long as I didn't try to sing. I had a grand time and practiced the piano three hours a day.

In my piano class, there were a group of women who had been paying their two dollars a semester and taking from Mr. Clark for eight years. Every month, they had a 'play for each other potluck' at one of their houses. They invited me to join them.

My first time was an evening at Mrs. Cailliet's house where a ten-foot ebony Bechstein grand piano sat in her living room. After dinner, they began to play. I tried to be cool, to act like an adult and not as giddy as I felt just being there. My eyes kept straying to one of my fellow students. There was a running debate in my head about how old she might be; it was hard to tell. She was beautiful and she had on a crimson full-skirted silk dress with a triple strand of matched thumb sized pearls around her neck. I had lived in the Orient, and was familiar enough with pearls to know that these were real. Finally, everyone turned to her and said, "Oh Imogene, play for us." She went to that huge shinning black piano, spread the yards of crimson silk out on the black bench, smiled graciously, and tore into George Gershwin. It was awesome!

The next day at school, I caught up with Mrs. Cailliet--as she, not only a concert pianist, was one of my professors. "Thank you so much for inviting me to dinner last night. I really enjoyed it."

Smiling, she said, "You are very welcome. The girls asked for you to come."

"Mrs. Cailliet, frankly, I feel intimidated where these women are concerned. Who is Imogene, that woman in the crimson dress who played last night?"

"You feel intimidated!" said Mrs. Cailliet. "That woman was in the Ziegfeld Follies! That woman took piano lessons from George Gershwin! That woman was on stage with Jack Benny! Intimidated! How do you think I feel?"

For some reason, these women decided to take me into their fold. Imogene took me to the King Tut exhibit in downtown L.A. with her exquisite daughter who was the mistress of a big network T.V. newsman. We had lunch in a restaurant by the museum and every male in there looked up and focused on the daughter when we walked in. "This is amazing," I muttered, as I had just finished Lewis Thomas' *Lives of a Cell*--a book that Mr. Clark had insisted we read. I was remembering Thomas' comments about maybe there are present today in Homo sapiens some leftover evolutionary bits like insect pheromones. *By golly!* I thought. *I might be seeing the reality of that at work on the males in this room.*

Margie, a fourteen year member of the Roger Wagner Chorale, took me downtown to the Dorothy Chandler Pavilion for my first opera and ballet. The opera was Carmen. I loved it and tried not to laugh as several people around me went to sleep in the second act; one man began to snore. Swan Lake, the ballet, was wonderful! We were in the third row and I was surprised at the sound of clopping from the wood blocks in the dancer's toe shoes.

I did the best I could in returning their friendship. My winner was soy sauce chicken from the Chinese cooking classes I took in Okinawa. They loved it. Margie was ecstatic. She called me the very next day to say it was already in the Jewish cookbooks of East Los Angeles and New York City.

These women became my friends and got me through the four years in California.

In L.A., Ronald seemed to be gone almost as much as he had been in the military. But here, it was just going to work early and getting home very late because we lived in the San Fernando Valley; and he worked in Santa Monica. Ronald was in marketing for Lear Seigler, I think missiles, with a $20,000 a year entertainment budget to keep his clients happy. Most of it was spent on the military when they came to the plant as they liked going to fancy restaurants and topless bars. R.D. would come home exhausted after having a night out at one of the finest restaurants in town, telling me about the movie stars at the adjoining tables.

Becky, Wendy, Kevin, and I managed just fine; we were good at it. Being a military family was excellent training, although I had reason to be both grateful, and amused, when my neighbor's husband, who had come to my rescue in several wild situations, limited his comments to, "It has been an interesting experience living next door to you."

Later, after going along on one of Ronald's business conferences in Washington, D.C., I dropped down to Englewood, Florida, to see Mom and Dad. There I found an old house on the inland waterway that smelled bad. My realtor said no one would ever buy it. "Ronald, it's on the inland waterway south of the bridge to Manasota Key. I don't even know how many bedrooms it has. I just walked in the front door and out the back," I said on the phone that evening. "I don't care if we have to pitch a tent in the back yard. I want that view."

To my surprise, as I was thinking of renting the house and moving there when he retired, again--Ronald jumped at the chance to leave California. Within six weeks, we had sold our house and arrived in Englewood.

Manasota Key, a barrier island, was on the other side of our inland waterway. It had wonderful beaches. When we got there in 1978, you could walk the sand for miles in the summer and not see a person. These islands were summer nesting grounds for the endangered Loggerhead Turtle. I became a volunteer monitor holding, under federal and state law, the Loggerhead Turtle permit in my county for the next ten years. This time, I had fallen in love with a state.

Florida, in 1987, was beginning their Comprehensive Planning Process. Tom Pellem, head of the Department of Community Affairs (DCA), was coming to Sanibel Island--the barrier island almost a 100 miles south of Englewood--to hold the first DCA state planners' workshop. I loved these beaches. Like a puppy dog, I was curious and wanted to go. When I asked if I could, I was told yes; but, it was for planners and would probably get technical. Braced to be overwhelmed, I went, the only 'just plain citizen' there. At the big opening session, our new planners were asked how long they had been in Florida--very few had been here over a year. They were from places like Connecticut, Michigan, and New York with little knowledge about the real Florida.

Oh Boy! Are we in trouble, I thought. I knew the difference as I had already taken some classes in barrier island beaches, and a Biology class at Manatee Community College where my term paper was on the "Salt Handling Properties of the Red, Black, and White Mangrove." Having been one of the people in Charlotte County who started our Native Plant Society, I understood that you shouldn't plan for Florida without knowing how this place works. We were different. I had laughed when a senator from Sarasota facetiously suggested that Florida have a concentration-like camp where newcomers had to stay until they learned how to live here without doing damage. After two days in Sanibel, I began to take that suggestion seriously. At one workshop the instructor said, "Now, I'm going to get really technical." *Shit! Here it comes. I'm going to be embarrassed,* I thought sinking down in my chair. Then he said, "How many people here know what a red mangrove is?" Two people raised their hands; I was one. Thankfully, I had been taking notes. In concern, I sent them to Pat Drago, the Natural Resources Director of the League of Women Voters of Florida.

Perhaps that is where it all started, I'm not certain. Later, Pat--a visionary-- worried about what was going to happen to our beaches with the coming impact of people and development. She decided to get the League ready with a state-wide Beaches and Shores study. Pat asked me to write the environmental part. They expected, I knew, the usual typed report. Florida's coasts and beaches were one of my passions. I wanted badly to do well, to present this information so people would both enjoy and understand it. Since I had no experience in this kind of thing, I simply did something from my heart, a little more visual and conversational, like the newsletters that I had been putting out for the Native Plant Society.

The League liked my effort. Later, they got a grant and had it published.

When Pat resigned as Natural Resources Director, the state board asked me to step in. In the four years that followed, I would occasionally meet someone who on hearing my name would say, "I loved that coastal pamphlet. You are the reason I joined the League."

As Natural Resources Director, the Growth Management Portfolio was another of my responsibilities from 1987 to 1991. These were important and interesting years for Florida. The conversation was about quality of life. Many people believed that this was our chance; we could save Florida; we could get some control of the state's exploding growth. The League insisted that our members get involved in every county where we had an organization. Part of my job was to 'drum up the troops;' and we poured volunteers into the process. Women from all over this state called me, some of them crying, "Sue, we're losing everything. The developers will destroy us. What can we do?"

"Sue, I have been sitting on my bed for hours trying to read this stuff. Do I have to? This is awful and so boring."

"Sue, there are so many meetings, and I don't understand a thing. Do I have to go?"

"Sue, I'm so depressed."

I got really depressed too. Until one day it occurred to me that through this process the average citizen was learning about their government and who really governs. Then I started to laugh. This is turning into a civic education class about how local government works! *Good for Florida*, I thought.

That was before DCA started to make all those settlement agreements with lawyers and developers, as far as the environmental community was concerned, behind closed doors. The development continued unabated with not enough control, and, because the law said you were to require infrastructure concurrent with development, just more expensive. A lot of the excitement became cynical as local government and the little citizen already living in Florida got stuck with the costs.

Sometime in here, R.D. and I were going out for dinner with friends. He was driving the big old Buick we just got from the bank and two other couples were in the back of the car. The women were talking about someone's horrible personal situation. I was shocked and turned to find out what on earth was going on; who were they talking about? It was the T.V. show Dallas, which I had never seen.

That was it. I couldn't live like this. I had to do something. So I asked a diverse group of women I had met here and there to lunch. The one stipulation was that what we talked about could not be personal. They just exploded into going over issues: politics, the cost of government, and the environment--as hungry as I was for good conversation. We started having lunch once a month. This is the group that not only decided that I was to run for county commissioner; they got me elected.

Running for elective office takes a certain personality, and I don't have it. I took such an aversion to parades that I decided if I'm ever in one again, I'm going to be ashes in a box. My first time out to campaign, my group had me going to Port Charlotte to the Saturday Flea Market. I drove out of Englewood about 7 a.m. Saturday morning deciding, as I managed the car and coffee, that I had lost my mind. I had never been to a flea market and never intended to go to one. Now, they had me standing in front of a booth hawking pamphlets and myself, and shaking hands with strangers, for two days.

What an experience that was! This was 1992, the year Perot ran, and some historians would call it the 'year of the women.' In the flea market, I stopped people as they tried to walk by me, putting a pamphlet in their hands, saying all the things a candidate says. Most of these people were country people: she, in an ironed cotton dress, he, in blue jeans with a Perot cap on his head, chewing something. She would clasp one of my hands in both of hers, and say, "Oh Honey, I'm so glad." He would say, "Little Lady, what can we do?" I adored them.

It's common for people to try to 'get' a politician when they are speaking in public. And Charlotte County had a lot of retired General Motor's workers. One evening, I was talking to a difficult group when a man started to heckle me and then wanted to know what kind of car I drove. I just laughed. What an opportunity to tell a story and kill some time. "You obviously haven't seen what I drive," I said to a restive audience. "It's an old diesel Buick with an obstinate personality. We got it for $2,000 from a bank that had repossessed it. I have to start it by taking the hose off the air handler on top of the motor, and spraying it with WD-40. Last year, when I was Natural Resources Director of the state League of Women Voters, I was in a motel in north Florida for one of our two-day board meetings. A policeman came to the door of my room at 2 a.m. to inform me someone had tried to steal my car. He escorted me out to see it. The car was in the center of the parking lot, one window broken and wires sticking out of the steering column. 'Mrs. Dudley,' he said, 'I'm sorry about the mess in your car. They tried to steal it, but something must have happened and they couldn't.' I just hoo-hawed. 'Well,' the policeman said looking at me as if I were strange, 'I've seen a lot of reactions to having someone try to steal your car, but this is a new one.' You don't understand about my car, I said, gasping for breath as I pictured the thief's frustration. They couldn't figure out how to start it." The crowd loved it. Charlotte County had had a female commissioner in 1974; I was their second.

Ronald didn't make it to my installation as county commissioner.

My obsession, four years ago, with the responsibility of that LWV coastal information effort ignited an incident that probably, and without my understanding at that time, changed my life. I drove R.D. crazy: "Why couldn't I do it right? I was stupid. Why was I taking all this time and putting so much work in this silly thing?" He came unglued he was so angry.

I ended up crying helplessly in front of him. "Ronald, you can't do this to me," I said between sobs. "I'm not paid money. The only thing I have is my pride in what I do. I won't let you take that away from me."

R.D. had been gone a lot. He was working as a realtor in Sarasota County. I knew he was unhappy but thought that if I left him alone, he could solve his problems. We had started to see a male counselor who told me it would be best if I did not talk to anyone about what was going on. At one session, I asked this counselor if he thought R.D. was going to get a divorce; and he said on a scale of 1 to 10 he would say it was a 9. I started to sob, and left his office. The counselor was upset and called Ronald to get me to come back. I refused.

Then I began crying like I did when Wendy severed his thumb. It was just a quiet, constant flow of tears, but only at certain times. It continued for a long time. I couldn't read a book or listen to music; and it was guaranteed to start when I drove a car.

I gave up books and music, but driving was a problem. The solution turned out to be another one of my funnies. Several years before, the local LWV had gotten me put on the county's Land Development Regulation Committee to our new Comprehensive Plan. I was the citizen dodo in the group with all the lawyers and developers; it was quite an education. One developer in particular was, in my mind, a really bad guy; and he thought I was a pest. These men ignored me so much that they let me keep my tape recorder going all the time. I got those tapes out and started listening to them again in my car. The tears would stop flowing the minute a tape started playing. I was nastily pleased. My developer nemesis would be real upset if he found out he had helped save my sanity.

Ronald left in 1994; and I finally told the children. (We were divorced in 2003.)

The group of women friends who had quietly stepped into my life--coming from the campaign, the turtle patrol, the Native Plant Society, the Unitarian Church--became my stability, and my base. My Ozark Hills background said I owed them. But the reality is we put into place a level of trust and support that has allowed all of us to be very proud of our ability to survive and grow. I sat between Brenda and her husband at their divorce; she cried on one shoulder, and he cried on the other. Brenda is our talented entrepreneurial business person. Marley, our artist, and I have worked on so many things together; now she mothers all of us. I was with Cindy at her divorce; and we all saw her into the Peace Corps and then back from Africa to her job, again, as Utility Director of North Port. One Gail ran my campaign, she is the real reason I got elected; she comes down every winter from Canada. Another Gail is a lawyer, educator, and talented photographer. Marilyn has become a minister, and a Chaplain, in an emotional growth that has amazed us all. "What can you say of a friend that lets you, when your husband can't handle it, put your dead cat in her freezer for the weekend," Brenda said, explaining to someone why they had decided to call themselves FOS: Friends of Sue.

Then in 1999, when I was sixty-four, I sold my home and moved to Gainesville. Chanting my new mantra "Why not?" Why not!" I resurrected my dream of forty-seven years ago. Finally, I would have a degree; but this one would be focused on the environment, and from the University of Florida. As Ronald had left me three years before, FOS just snickered when I told my hairdresser of fifteen years, "Richard, I'm leaving my husband here, but I'll be damned if I will leave you; I'm coming back every month." For these past eight years, FOS has happily put together the monthly weekends that we have all used for support, energy, and renewal.

In 2003, I graduated, at the age of 68, from the University of Florida with a Bachelor of Arts in Environment, Economics, and Policy from the School of Natural Resources and Environment. Some of my family, Kevin, Becky, Mike, and granddaughter, Ariel, Cousin Marc, his wife, Jan, and my brother Linn came. So did FOS. I was hyper--as they had threatened to hang a banner from the balcony saying, "Go Grandma!" But they didn't; they just shouted, and jumped up and down, and waved.

Sue Coffman Dudley
Gainesville, FL
2007

Hoo Ray!!! Gainesville, FL 2003

Sue Coffman Dudley

Sue at 18. Mizzou, 1953

Wedding Day. Phoenix, 1955

At home in Newfoundland. Stephenville, 1960

Kevin, Becky, Wendy in Stillwater. Oklahoma, 1963

ON THE ROAD AGAIN

Becky, Wendy and flower girl. Okinawa, 1966

Bomb Squad at our home Kakazu Ridge, 1967

A Grandma gift: 2 snook and a laugh! Englewood, 1971

Retirement Dayton, 1974

Commissioner Dudley Florida, 1992

Author's Notes

The Beginning

P. 2 - Several months before my request to go to summer school in Arizona, I had arrived home with a young man from Mizzou, who was a Catholic, wearing his fraternity pin. He thought he was in love and pushing to have a special Lambda Chi Alpha/Zeta Tau Alpha pinning ceremony for us before summer. I insisted on waiting until fall. Looking back at my strangely silent parents, I remember, suspiciously, that Flat River didn't even have a Catholic church.

P. 3 - In 2007, I was diagnosed with a genetic disease: Ankylosing spondylitis. My brother, Linn, had been diagnosed several years before. Ankylosing spondylitis is a member of the arthritis family--but with AS your bones want to fuse. With this disease, the more active you are the less you hurt. AS can show up as a low grade fever, heart murmur, and joint pain.

P. 7, 8 - In Florida, years later, I began to understand my mother. She told me that in bed every night my father would tell her what she was to do the next day--and she did it. In her new world, a small trailer on the inland waterway in Englewood, my mother found herself. She was really a naturalist, and, like her father, a dedicated fly fisherman. One evening, I sat at their small kitchen table watching my mother as she watched T.V. The program was *Blithe Spirit* on Hallmark Hall of Fame. My mother laughed and laughed. I could not remember my mother laughing...

DEFCON II
P. 28 - Stephenville sat on a plateau beside Newfoundland's Bay St. George with the Long Range Mountains to the east. The Long Range Mountains on Newfoundland's west coast are the northeastern most extension of our Appalachian Mountains. The 'International Appalachian Trail' now goes through that area.

WENDY
P. 47 - Pierce Jr College, LA., 1975--I began to understand what Wendy went through with transferring from his right to his left hand when I attended a lecture by Betty Edwards based on her doctorate. Her work would later be published as the book: Drawing On the Right Side of the Brain. Edwards talked about, and showed us slides of, the testing done on the 'split brain patients' of the later 1960s that gave some of the first insights into the connections, and the specializations, of the right and left brains. The left-brain has speech. Its mode of processing information is verbal and analytic; it is very good at planning. The right-brain's mode of processing information is non-verbal and global; it is rapid, complex, whole-pattern, spatial, and perceptual. Usually, one or the other is dominant. Left-brain dominance is shown by being right-handed; right-brain

dominance by being left-handed. (At the end of Edwards' lecture, she asked that anyone who was left-handed and had a left-handed mother go to UCLA to be tested. They were finding some of these people with the speech center in the Right Brain.)

Wendy, a right-hander, had been *forced* to the left-hand. He is, today, ambidextrous, and very good at testing new computer programs.

AFTERWARDS
P. 101,102 - Soy Sauce Chicken
Chicken (I use thighs without skin.)   2-2 1/2 lbs

Sauce:
2/3 cup soy sauce (Kikkoman is good.)
4 slices ginger
2 tbsp. wine
1/2 to 2/3 cups sugar
2 cups water
A few pieces of aniseed (Aniseed gives you the flavor!)

Combine sauce ingredients and heat to boiling. Put in chicken. Cover, cook for 10 minutes. Remove cover, lower heat; turn and baste chicken occasionally. Add a few tbsp. of water if necessary. Cook about 20 minutes per pound. Sauce should be reduced to about 1 cup, and it will be thick.

Garnish & Enjoy!
2 green onions slivered. Arrange chicken pieces on platter; garnish with green onion and pour sauce over chicken and onion. Serve hot or cold. (The sauce is good over rice. The chicken is great cold for picnics, or lunch, or just eating.)